# Business Idioms in America

## Bruce Stirling

Cover by Bruce Stirling
Layout and design by Bruce Stirling
3D USA Flag Map with states © Ermek @ shutterstock.com
Statue of Liberty and Flag © etraveler @ shutterstock.com
Made-in-USA stamp © DinoZ @ shutterstock.com
New York City Skyline silhouette © vladmark @ shutterstock.com

### Editors

Patricia Stirling, Gretchen Anderson, Kateryna Kucher, Renata C. T. Rabacov,
Eddie Carillo

For permission to use material from this text in any form, please forward your request to info@novapress.net.

**Disclaimer:** The characters in this text are works of fiction. Any likeness to any actual person is coincidental.

ISBN-10: 1889057967

ISBN-13: 9781889057965

## Published by *Nova Press*
9058 Lloyd Place
West Hollywood, CA
USA 90069
1-800-949-6175
info@novapress.net
www.novapress.net

# Contents

# How to Use this Book

*Business Idioms in America* consists of twenty lessons. Combined, they describe a day-in-the-life of a Joan Austen, a rising star in the advertising business in New York City. Each lesson stands alone as a single unit of study. However, it is best to work your way through from beginning to end. By doing so, you will follow Joan and her staff as they deal with myriad business and personal challenges. You will also be able to recycle idioms from one lesson to the next. Recycling idioms will help you remember and apply those idioms to future lessons and in real-world business situations.

## Format

Each lesson consists of seven steps. Each step has been designed to help you develop the English skills you need to communicate proficiently in any English-speaking business environment. The seven steps are as follows.

1 ➔ **Main Dialogue** - Each lesson starts with a main dialogue. The main dialogue introduces a business-related conflict that is resolved by Joan and her staff. In the main dialogue, 15 common business idioms/phrases/words are introduced.

2 ➔ **Definitions** - This section defines the 15 idioms/phrases/words introduced in the main dialogue.

3 ➔ **Practice** - This section is a fill-in-the-blanks exercise using the 15 idioms/phrases/words.

4 ➔ **The Story Continues** - In this section, the story introduced in the main dialogue continues. The characters might expand the topic or they might switch to a new topic. After you finish reading, you will answer questions.

5 ➔ **Expansion** - This section expands the topic in the main dialogue with 20 topically-related business idioms/phrases/words. This section is a multiple-choice test.

6 ➔ **Writing Practice** - For this section, you will write 15 separate sentences. Each sentence will use one of the 15 idioms/phrases/words introduced in the main dialogue and/or the expansion (step 5).

7 ➔ **More Writing Practice** - For this section, you will write a short passage using as many idioms/phrases/words from the lesson studied.

## Shakespeare (S)

William Shakespeare (1564-1616) was an English poet and playwright. He is considered the greatest writer in the English language. We all know his plays. The most famous are *Romeo and Juliet* and *Hamlet*. What, you ask, is Shakespeare doing in a book about business idioms? That, indeed, is the $64,000.00 question.

The answer is simple: Shakespeare added over 5,000 words, phrases and idioms to the English language. Many are still widely used, such as *to budge not an inch*, which means *cannot be moved or persuaded*, for example:

> <u>Mary</u>:   Hey, Dave. Did you ask the boss for a raise?
>
> <u>Dave</u>:   I did. But he wouldn't budge an inch.

Because you cannot learn English without learning Shakespeare, I have included in each lesson a famous Shakespearean idiom or phrase that is applicable to business English today. That idiom or phrase is indicated by (S).

## Okay, so what is an idiom?

An idiom is a comparison. Let me explain. Look at the following examples.

> 1. Jack eats like a wolf.
> 2. Jack is as hungry as a wolf.
> 3. Hey, wolfman! How are you? Long time, no see!
> 4. Jack's an animal. The guy's crazy.

In examples 1 and 2, I am comparing Jack to a wolf. A wolf is a wild animal and when hungry, watch out! When I say, "Jack is as hungry as a wolf," I am speaking (writing) figuratively. Is my friend Jack a real (literal) wolf? No. Instead, I am figuratively (idiomatically) comparing him to a wolf to create a picture in your mind. That picture emphasizes the degree of Jack's hunger. How hungry is Jack? As hungry as a wolf. As you can see, an idiom is a comparison that paints a figurative picture using words.

In examples 3 and 4, I am still figuratively (idiomatically) comparing Jack to an animal. However, I am not using the comparatives like or as. This kind of idiomatic comparison (not using like or as) is called an indirect comparison or a *metaphor* (met-ah-for). A metaphor is an implied (suggested) comparison. Notice how in examples 1 and 2, I do use like and as. This kind of idiomatic comparison is called a direct comparison or a *simile* (sim-ah-lee).

### <u>Remember</u> ➜ An idiom is either a metaphor or a simile.

How do you know if what you are reading, saying or hearing is an idiom or not? Look for the comparison. If there is a comparison (a simile or a metaphor), then it is an idiom. If there is no comparison (no simile or metaphor), it is not an idiom. If it sounds like an idiom—but there is no comparison—it is probably a common expression, a prepositional phrase, a literal phrasal verb, or slang.

And that, in a nutshell, is the skinny on idioms. It's time to get the show on the road. For definitions, remember to check the word list starting on page 188.

*Bruce Stirling*

## Characters

**Joan Austen**
- ✓ owner and CEO of Austen Advertising, New York City
- ✓ age 50, divorced; one child, three dogs, two cats
- ✓ B.A. in Business, Yale, summa cum laude

**Maria Perez**
- ✓ Ms. Austen's executive assistant
- ✓ age 29, single
- ✓ studying part-time for her M.B.A. in marketing at NYU

**Don Reed**
- ✓ attorney; partner in a Manhattan law firm
- ✓ age 51, divorced; two children, one dog, one grandchild
- ✓ J.D., LL.M., Harvard Law, magna cum laude

**Judy Hart**
- ✓ managing director of Austen Advertising
- ✓ age 46, married; two children, two cats
- ✓ M.B.A. in Marketing, UMass, cum laude

**Sara O'Reilly**
- ✓ CFO of Austen Advertising
- ✓ age 55, married; four children, six grandchildren
- ✓ M.B.A. in Finance, UConn, magna cum laude

**Beth Faraz**
- ✓ creative director of Austen Advertising
- ✓ age 44, married; two children, parrot, rabbit
- ✓ M.F.A. in Digital Media, Rhode Island School of Design

**Jake Gittes**
- ✓ senior account executive at Austen Advertising
- ✓ age 39, married; three cats
- ✓ M.F.A. in Writing, Vermont College

**Bob Catelin**
- ✓ owner and CEO of Bobcat Organic Beer
- ✓ age 60, married; three children, ten grandchildren
- ✓ high-school drop out; Viet Nam veteran

**Rick Royce**
- ✓ copywriter at Austen Advertising
- ✓ age 31, single
- ✓ USC, B.A. in Cinematic Arts

**Debra Lynde**
- ✓ copywriter at Austen Advertising
- ✓ age 34, single; LSU, B.A. in History

**Hector Gomez**
- ✓ IT manager at Austen Advertising
- ✓ age 30, single; B.A. in Computer Science, FSU

**Steve Palmia**
- ✓ junior account executive at Austen Advertising
- ✓ age 28, single
- ✓ B.A. in Business, SUNY Brooklyn

**Talita Alves**
- ✓ age 22, single
- ✓ third-year student, The Architecture Institute, NYC

# Lesson #1 ➜ *Stuck in Traffic*

➜ **8:30 a.m.** Joan Austen is driving on I-95* from her home in Greenwich, Connecticut to her office in Manhattan. She calls her office and talks to her executive assistant Maria Perez.

❋ ❋ ❋

Maria: Good morning, Austen Advertising, Maria Perez speaking. How can I help you?

Joan: Hi, Maria. It's Joan. I'm <u>stuck in traffic</u>. A truck flipped over in the other lane and is blocking traffic. I can't believe it. I leave home two hours early <u>to beat the traffic</u> and look what happens.

Maria: Are you even moving?

Joan: Barely. Everyone is <u>rubbernecking</u>. *(honking her horn)* C'mon, people! <u>Put a fire under it</u>! *(to Maria)* Did Rick Meyers call?

Maria: He did. Ten minutes ago.

Joan: What's <u>the bottom line</u>?

Maria: You <u>sealed the deal</u>.

Joan: Really?

Maria: He said you <u>hit it out of the park</u>. He loves your new idea. He said, and I quote, "Austen Advertising really <u>went to bat for us</u>."

Joan: I should hope so. We <u>pulled out all the stops</u> <u>to bring his campaign in under budget</u>. What about Mario Biagi? Did he call?

Maria: Yes. Suffice it to say, Mr. Pizza is <u>not a happy camper</u>. He wants you <u>to work up some new ideas</u> by tomorrow.

Joan: By tomorrow? Great. <u>Back to the drawing board</u>. Tell everyone we're going to have <u>a working lunch</u>, okay? Order lots of veggie wraps and <u>hold the mayo on mine</u>. And cancel my eight o'clock. Tell Bert Howe I got hung up in traffic. Ask him if we can hook up tomorrow at the same time.

Maria: Done and done.

---

\* I-95    *Interstate Highway 95. The main north-south artery that connects all major east coast cities from Boston to Miami.*

## 1.A ➜ Definitions

1) *stuck in traffic (to be)*
   - to be in a vehicle but not moving due to heavy traffic/accident

2) *beat the traffic (to)*
   - to avoid rush-hour by leaving early

3) *rubberneck (to)*
   - to slow down and look at an accident

4) *put a fire under it (to)*
   - to hurry up; to get moving

5) *bottom line (the)*
   - the message; the conclusion

6) *seal the deal (to)*
   - to come to an agreement

7) *hit it out of the park (to)*
   - to hit a homerun; to think of a great idea; to succeed beyond expectation

8) *go to bat for someone (to)*
   - to support a friend/colleague/cause

9) *pull out all the stops (to)*
   - to do whatever is necessary to succeed

10) *bring something in under budget (to)*
    - to complete a project, etc., below the budgeted cost

11) *happy camper (to be not a)*
    - a person who is not happy

12) *work up something (to)*
    - to develop ideas; to brainstorm

13) *go back to the drawing board (to)*
    - to rethink; to start over

14) *working lunch (a)*
    - working during lunch

15) *hold something (to)*
    - to not include; to leave off/out

## 1.B → Practice

**Task** → Fill in the blanks using the idioms on the previous page.

1.  Bob got up early because he wanted _____ .

2.  When you are _____ , you have no choice but to sit and wait it out.

3.  Al is _____ . He just learned that he is going to be let go.

4.  After Joan and Alexander _____ , they celebrated with dinner and a Broadway show.

5.  Yurica is always _____ the homeless.

6.  When people slow down _____ , they often cause fender benders.

7.  When Carol ordered a hamburger, she told the server _____ the onions.

8.  To meet the deadline, the team had _____ .

9.  Maria never fails _____ a project _____ .

10. Joan wanted Rick _____ a new slogan by tomorrow.

11. Carla has arranged to have _____ with the new client.

12. After the prototype failed, the team had _____ .

13. In business, making a profit is _____ .

14. Bob's last idea was terrible, but this time he _____ .

15. Steve told the lazy intern _____ .

## 1.C ➜ The Story Continues

**Task** ➜ Read the rest of the conversation, then answer the questions.

Maria:    Anything else, Joan?

Joan:    Nothing for now. I'll see you when I get in.

Maria:    Have you thought about what we talked about?

Joan:    Thought about what?

Maria:    You know, my raise.

Joan:    Right. Sorry, I have so much on my plate, it slipped my mind.

Maria:    You said I'm in line for one.

Joan:    I did. But we're facing a budget crunch. The move to a bigger office is going to eat into our cash flow.

Maria:    So that means no raise?

Joan:    Not necessarily. Let's circle back to it when I get in, okay?

## Questions

1. How many idioms can you identify in the passage above? Compare your choices to those on pg. 156. For definitions, see the word list, pg. 188.

2. Did Maria get what she wanted? Explain.

3. What is the traffic like in your country? Do you prefer to drive to work, take public transportation, go by bike or on foot? Explain.

4. In your country, how often do employees get a raise? What is the procedure for getting a raise? Explain.

5. Verbally summarize this lesson. Time yourself. You have 2 minutes.

## 2.A → Definitions

1) *icing on the cake (the)*
   - the best part; the added benefit

2) *shingle (a)*
   - traditionally a wooden sign advertising a law practice

3) *rub elbows (with someone) (to)*
   - to socialize with the purpose of making connections; to schmooze

4) *heavy hitter (a)*
   - a person with power and influence

5) *take a rain check (to)*
   - to promise to do another time

6) *schmoozer (a)*
   - one who socializes for personal gain

7) *burn the midnight oil (to)*
   - to work late often to meet a deadline

8) *in the market for something (to be)*
   - to be looking to buy or rent

9) *burst at the seams (to)*
   - to break open and overflow

10) *ramp up (to)*
    - to increase in speed

11) *scuttlebutt (the)*
    - the latest rumor(s)/gossip

12) *heads up (the)*
    - the information/warning/notice

13) *in this neck of the woods*
    - in this neighborhood/town/city

14) *through the roof (to be)*
    - to be very expensive

15) *run the numbers (to)*
    - to do financial calculations

## 2.B ➜ Practice

**Task** ➜ Fill in the blanks using the idioms on the previous page.

1.  Anne is _____ a new house.

2.  Apple had _____ production to meet the Christmas demand.

3.  _____ , you'll always get stuck in traffic.

4.  Before you seal a deal, you had better _____ first.

5.  _____ is the boss is not a happy camper.

6.  Don pulled out all the stops to get his name on _____ .

7.  The bottom line is our cash flow is _____ .

8.  The auditors are coming? Really? Thanks for _____ .

9.  Adriana had _____ to meet the morning deadline.

10. In Hollywood, Stephen Spielberg is definitely _____ .

11. This subway system is so old, it is _____ .

12. Linda is such _____ . She'll do anything to seal the deal.

13. Frank loves _____ heavy hitters.

14. Jason got a raise and a promotion. He really hit it out of the park this time.
    The _____ is his new corner office.

15. I can't make the working lunch, sorry. I'll have to _____ .

## 2.C ➜ The Story Continues

**Task** ➜ Read the rest of the conversation, then answer the questions.

Don:    Just for the record, the party starts at eight.

Joan:   How can I turn a profit if I'm always out tripping the light fantastic?

Don:    An evening away from work is not going to sink the ship.

Joan:   I don't know. I need incentive. Make me an offer.

Don:    Consider it a tax write-off.

Joan:   Taxes? Bor-ing. Can't you sweeten the deal?

Don:    All right. Marry me.

Joan:   Marry you? Hmmm. Interesting. Is that your final offer? *

Don:    I'll tell you tonight. Bye.

*(Don exits from the elevator.)*

## Questions

1. How many idioms can you identify in the passage above? What does each mean? Compare your choices to those on pg. 157. For definitions, see the word list, pg. 188.

2. Do you think Joan will go to the party? Why? Why not? Explain.

3. Are you a schmoozer? Explain.

4. Talk about real estate prices in your country. How do they compare to prices in the United States? Explain.

5. Verbally summarize this lesson. Time yourself. You have <u>2</u> minutes.

*\* See Movie-TV quotes pg. 214*

## 2.D ➜ Expansion

**Task** ➜ Match the expressions in column A with the definitions in column B.

**A**       **B**

1) piece of cake (a) ____
2) conundrum (a) ____
3) crunch the numbers (to) ____
4) on the market (to be) ____
5) bonus (a) ____
6) out of the woods (to be) ____
7) rumormonger (a) ____
8) burn the candle at both ends (to) ___
9) hit the roof (to) ____
10) yes-man (a) ____
11) climb the corporate ladder (to) ____
12) go back to square one (to) ____
13) shot in the arm (a) ____
14) in the bag (to be) ____
15) in a pickle (to be) (S) ____
16) start from scratch (to) ____
17) shop around (to) ____
18) peddle (to) ____
19) labor of love (a) ____
20) in a New-York minute ____

A) a mystery/problem/puzzle
B) to sell/promote/pitch
C) one who always agrees with the boss
D) guaranteed
E) as easy as pie
F) one who spreads rumors; a gossip
G) done for love not money or gain
H) to advance in a company through promotions
I) to be out of danger
J) to do financial calculations; to run the numbers
K) to burn the midnight oil
L) to be very upset or angry
M) to look for a better deal
N) to be available for purchase
O) instantly; immediately
P) to be in a difficult position
Q) a stimulus
R) to start over from the beginning
S) incentive; reward for performing well
T) to start with basic resources

## 2.E ➜ Writing Practice

**Task** ➜ Write a sentence using each idiom.

1) icing on the cake (the)

_____

2) peddle (to)

_____

3) shop around (to)

_____

4) heavy hitter (a)

_____

5) take a rain check (to)

_____

6) schmoozer (a)

_____

7) burn the midnight oil (to)

_____

8) in the market for something (to be)

_____

9) in a New-York minute

_____

10) crunch the numbers (to)

_____

11) scuttlebutt (the)

_____

12) heads up (the)

_____

13) in this neck of the woods

_____

14) through the roof (to be)

_____

15) climb the corporate ladder (to)

_____

## 2.F ➜ More Writing Practice

**Task** ➜ Write a short passage using as many idioms as you can from this lesson. The topic is your choice. Make it business-related if possible.

_____

_____

_____

_____

_____

_____

_____

_____

# Lesson #3 ➜ *An In*

➜ **9:35 a.m.** Sara and Judy wait for their weekly meeting with Joan in the conference room. Sara and Judy are discussing *Art Advertising*, a competitor.

✳ ✳ ✳

Sara: Have you seen Art's new TV ad for Morgan Financial?

Judy: I have. What <u>a dog</u>. I wonder who dreamed that one up? I wouldn't want to be in that guy's shoes.

Sara: Can you believe it? Two years ago, Art Advertising was <u>eating our lunch</u>. They were <u>the 800-pound gorilla</u>. Since then they've <u>gone off the rails</u>.

Judy: I've heard they <u>cleaned house</u> and brought in <u>new blood</u>. Don't quote me, but I've also heard that General Motors is headed our way.

Sara: GM is leaving Art? No way. Maybe we should send out some feelers. Let's put Jake on it. He's our best pitch man.

Judy: Relax. <u>I've got it covered</u>. I'm having lunch with John Phillips, GM's vice president of marketing. We went to UMass together. We even dated for a while, so I definitely <u>have an in</u>.

Sara: Small world.

Judy: You know what they say: What goes around, comes around.

Sara: So how much do we <u>stand to gain</u> if GM <u>jumps ship</u>?

Judy: I did some <u>back-of-the-envelope calculations</u>.

Sara: And?

Judy: If we <u>land GM</u>, we stand to make ten million at the very least. And that's just for starters. If GM jumps ship, others are sure to follow. If that happens, believe me, <u>the sky is the limit</u>.

Sara: Does Joan know about this?

Joan: *(entering)* Sorry I'm late. Traffic was a nightmare. So, what's with Mr. Pizza? Why's Mario Biagi <u>having kittens</u>?

Sara: You'd better talk to Jake about it.

Joan: Right. Judy, you <u>look like the cat that ate the canary</u>. Good news, I hope.

## 3.A → Definitions

1)  *dog (a)*
    - a bad idea; a poor performer
    _____

2)  *eat one's lunch (to)*
    - to take away market share; to have a competitive advantage
    _____

3)  *800-pound gorilla (the)*
    - the dominant player in a market
    _____

4)  *go off the rails (to)*
    - to lose focus; to act strange
    _____

5)  *clean house (to)*
    - to fire/lay off employees
    _____

6)  *new blood*
    - new employees; new talent
    _____

7)  *have (got) it covered (to)*
    • to take control/action
    _____

8)  *have an in (to)*
    - to have a connection with influence
    _____

9)  *stand to gain (to)*
    - to benefit from
    _____

10) *jump ship (to)*
    - to leave suddenly
    _____

11) *back-of-the-envelope calculations*
    - a rough estimate on paper
    _____

12) *land something (to)*
    - to get/win something
    _____

13) *sky is the limit (the)*
    - unlimited opportunities
    _____

14) *have kittens (to)*
    - to express extreme worry/fear
    _____

15) *look like the cat that ate the canary (to)*
    - to look self-satisfied/pleased
    _____

## 3.B → Practice

**Task** → Fill in the blanks using the idioms on the previous page.

1.  I've heard that movie is _____ real _____ .

2.  Google is _____ in the internet-search business.

3.  Elvia _____ because she got a better offer.

4.  Talita would love _____ a job at Austen Advertising.

5.  The company intends _____? Really? No, I hadn't heard.
    Thanks for the heads up.

6.  We are losing market share. Our competitors are _____ .

7.  The scuttlebutt is the CEO has _____ .

8.  Now that we've sealed the deal, _____ .

9.  Don't worry. I _____ . I just ran the numbers.

10. What do we _____ if we hire a heavy hitter?

11. The company is in the market for some _____ .

12. These _____ are through the roof.

13. Joe is such a schmoozer. I swear, he _____ everywhere.

14. Joan is _____ because we forgot to work up
    some ideas.

15. "Why does Anne _____?" Brian asked.
    Because," Dave replied, "she brought the project in under budget."

## 3.C → The Story Continues

**Task** → Read the rest of the conversation, then answer the questions.

Judy: Great news. I'm having lunch with John Phillips, GM's V.P. of marketing. The buzz is GM is leaving Art Advertising and Mr. Phillips wants to be, and I quote, "Brought up to speed on Austen Advertising."

Joan: That's fantastic.

Judy: Nothing is set in stone. This little tête-à-tête is just a trial balloon.

Joan: It doesn't matter. Pull out all the stops.

Judy: Believe me, I'm going to make him an offer he can't refuse.*

Joan: Where are you taking him?

Judy: He's taking me to that new French place, La Baguette. Have you been?

Joan: No. I'm off butter and cream.

Judy: Me too. But I'm willing to take one for the team if it means snagging GM.

## Questions

1. How many idioms can you identify in the passage above? What does each mean? Compare your choices to those on pg. 159. For definitions, see the word list, pg. 188.

2. How do you think Judy will pull out all the stops? Explain.

3. When looking for work, how important are connections in your country compared to the United States? Explain.

4. In your country, do business people meet and work over lunch? Explain.

5. Verbally summarize this lesson. Time yourself. You have <u>2</u> minutes.

*See Movie-TV quotes pg. 214*

## 3.D ➜ Expansion

**Task** ➜ Match the expressions in column A with the definitions in column B.

**A**

1) have an out (to) ____

2) clean up (to) ____

3) stand to lose (to) ____

4) have all the bases covered (to) ____

5) jump the gun (to) ____

6) "A" player (an) ____

7) shape up or ship out (to) ____

8) wishy-washy (to be) ____

9) It's a dog-eat-dog world. ____

10) hob knob (to) (S) ____

11) learn the ropes (to) ____

12) in the doghouse (to be) ____

13) jump the shark (to) ____

14) take the bull by the horns (to) ____

15) the canary in the coal mine ____

16) bite the bullet (to) ____

17) jump through the hoops (to) ____

18) pass the buck (to) ____

19) work out the kinks (to) ____

20) go overboard (to) ____

**B**

A) a heavy hitter

B) to learn the system

C) to face possible loss

D) a warning sign

E) to face many obstacles to reach a goal

F) to win decisively

G) to find and solve problems

H) to try too hard

I) My way or the highway.

J) the point at which something successful begins to go downhill; the beginning of the end

K) to avoid responsibility by giving it to someone else

L) to be out of favor/under a cloud

M) to have an exit strategy/excuse

N) to be prepared thoroughly

O) to rush to a wrong conclusion

P) to schmooze; to rub elbows with

Q) to accept a difficult challenge

R) to be uncertain/undecided

S) to make a difficult decision

T) everyone for themselves; no mercy

## 3.E ➜ **Writing Practice**

**Task** ➜ Write a sentence using each idiom.

1) dog (a)

_____

2) eat someone's lunch (to)

_____

3) 800-pound gorilla (the)

_____

4) go off the rails (to)

_____

5) clean house (to)

_____

6) new blood

_____

7) have (got) it covered (to)

_____

8) have an in (to)

_____

9) stand to gain (to)

_____

10) jump ship (to)

_____

11)  back-of-the-envelope calculations

_____

12)  land something (to)

_____

13)  sky is the limit (the)

_____

14)  have kittens (to)

_____

15)  look like the cat that ate the canary (to)

_____

## 3.F ➜ More Writing Practice

**Task** ➜ Write a short passage using as many idioms as you can from this
lesson. The topic is your choice. Make it business-related if possible.

_____

_____

_____

_____

_____

_____

_____

# Lesson #4 ➔ *A Bump in the Road*

➔ **10:35 a.m.** Joan works at her desk. Jake enters.

✱ ✱ ✱

Jake:    Hi, Joan. You wanted to see me?

Joan:    Jake, hi. Yes. Come in. We need to talk. Have a seat.

Jake:    I take it that this is about the Biagi account?

Joan:    Right. So, begin at the beginning.

Jake:    Well, it all started last November, just before Black Friday. Back then...

Joan:    Don't tell me the whole story. Just give me the gist, okay?

Jake:    Sure. The bottom line is Mario Biagi talks out of both sides of his mouth. He says he likes one idea, then two seconds later he turns around and throws cold water on it.

Joan:    He is the client, you know. He does have the final say.

Jake:    Joan, we have bent over backwards for him. He tells us to "Think outside the box." We do and he still flip-flops. So, is my head on the chopping block or what?

Joan:    Of course not. Relax. We'll flesh out some ideas during lunch, then run them by him.

Jake:    And if he gives us the-thumbs-down again?

Joan:    We'll cross that bridge when we come to it. In the meantime, we have to step up to the plate and give it our best shot. Biagi Pizza was my first big client. I don't want to lose it.

Jake:    What about the budget for shooting the Chanel ad?

Joan:    Sounds good.

Jake:    So, I've got the OK?

Joan:    Absolutely. Don't sell yourself short. You've got what it takes to get the job done. This is just a bump in the road.

Jake:    Thanks for the vote of confidence.

Joan:    Just make Mario Biagi happy. He's a cash cow.

## 4.A → Definitions

1) *I take it that...*
   - I assume that...

2) *Black Friday*
   - Thanksgiving Friday; a day of sales; the start of Christmas shopping

3) *gist (the)*
   - a brief summary; the bottom line

4) *talk out of both sides of one's mouth (to)*
   - to contradict oneself

5) *throw cold water on something (to)*
   - to reject with criticism

6) *bend over backwards (to)*
   - to try hard to please

7) *think outside the box (to)*
   - to think differently/originally

8) *flip-flop (to)*
   - to change one's position

9) *on the chopping block (to be)*
   - to be in serious trouble

10) *flesh out something (to)*
    - to develop/expand in detail

11) *run something by someone (to)*
    - to present for approval/feedback

12) *cross that bridge when one comes to it (to)*
    - to deal with a problem/issue at the time, not before

13) *step up to the plate (to)*
    - to take action/responsibility

14) *sell oneself short (to)*
    - to not believe in yourself/abilities

15) *cash cow (a)*
    - a reliable source of income from an established brand/product

## 4.B ➜ Practice

**Task** ➜ Fill in the blanks using the idioms on the previous page.

1.  The iPhone, the Big Mac and Diet Coke are all _____ .

2.  Jake wants to shoot a TV commercial on Mt. Everest. Joan, however, _____ _____ that idea and told him to go back to the drawing board.

3.  To seal the deal, the team really has _____ .

4.  Joan hired Sylvia because she always _____ . The woman is bursting at the seams with ideas.

5.  Josh is always late. The scuttlebutt is his head is _____ .

6.  When a politician says, "It's time to clean house!" you know she is _____ _____ .

7.  During their working lunch, Joan _____ some new ideas for a new client, a heavy hitter on Wall Street.

8.  Before you run the numbers, I want you _____ that idea _____ before I give you the OK.

9.  Don't worry about the Christmas party. It's only September. We'll _____ _____ .

10. Ewa speaks English perfectly, yet she is always _____ .

11. The team really _____ to make the client happy.

12. Stop _____ . Put a fire under it and hit one out of the park.

13. If someone says, "Just give me _____ ," she means, "I don't have time for the whole story. Just give me the bottom line."

14. I see you're not eating sushi. _____ you don't like Japanese food.

15. If you want the best deals on _____ , you had better not get stuck in traffic. By 5:00 a.m., retail stores are already bursting at the seams with customers.

## 4.C → The Story Continues

**Task** → Read the rest of the conversation, then answer the questions.

Joan:   Right. Moving on. How's Bobcat Beer doing? What's the latest?

Jake:   Steve is giving the owner the pitch at the brewery this morning.

Joan:   Good. How is the new man Steve doing?

Jake:   I had my doubts at first, but he's really pulled up his socks. As you know, he signed Office Station last week. They loved his pitch. I'm telling you, the guy is a natural. He hits all the right notes. We definitely lucked out when we landed him.

Joan:   That's good to hear. What about Bobcat Beer? Does it look like a done deal?

Jake:   I'll go out on a limb and say yes. Steve is a closer. He will get the account. In the meantime, keep your fingers crossed.

## Questions

1.  How many idioms can you identify in the passage above? What does each mean? Compare your choices to those on pg. 160. For definitions, see the word list, pg. 188.

2.  What is Jake's impression of Steve so far? Explain.

3.  Is it easy or difficult for you to pitch an idea? Explain.

4.  Being able to pitch an idea is an essential part of doing business. Why? Explain.

5.  Verbally summarize this lesson. Time yourself. You have 2 minutes.

## 4.D → Expansion

**Task** → Match the expressions in column A with the definitions in column B.

**A**

**B**

1)  Black Tuesday ____

2)  take a bath (to) ____

3)  go the extra mile (to) ____

4)  waffle (to) ____

5)  throw one under the bus (to) ____

6)  throw one a curve (to) ____

7)  throw in the towel (to) ____

8)  discombobulated (to be) ____

9)  on the block (to be) ____

10) blockbuster (a) ____

11) kick it up a notch (to) ____

12) cross the line (to) ____

13) wait until the cows come home (to) ____

14) swim with the sharks (to) ____

15) sacred cow (a) ____

16) beat a dead horse (to) ____

17) bark up the wrong tree (to) ____

18) hound (to) ____

19) What's done is done. (S) ____

20) throw the baby out with the bath water (to) ____

A)  to flip-flop

B)  to give up/surrender/capitulate

C)  to be confused/perplexed/flummoxed

D)  to sacrifice for personal gain

E)  water under the bridge

F)  to wait for a very long time

G)  to ask the wrong person; to move in the wrong direction

H)  to bother; to go after continually

I)  to continue to argue when debate is over

J)  to work with heavy hitters

K)  when eliminating a negative, a positive element is also eliminated; an avoidable error

L)  to be available for purchase

M)  to incur a large loss on an investment

N)  to bend over backwards for

O)  to introduce something new unexpectedly

P)  a big financial success

Q)  to take something to the next level

R)  to cross the point of no return

S)  untouchable; cannot be criticized

T)  October 29, 1929; the stock market crashed signaling the start of the Great Depression

## 4.E ➜ Writing Practice

**Task** ➜ Write a sentence using each idiom.

1)  I take it that...

_____

2)  go the extra mile (to)

_____

3)  gist (the)

_____

4)  beat a dead horse (to)

_____

5)  throw cold water on something (to)

_____

6)  bend over backwards (to)

_____

7)  think outside the box (to)

_____

8)  flip-flop (to)

_____

9)  on the chopping block (to be)

_____

10) flesh out something (to)

_____

11)  run something by someone (to)

_____

12)  cross that bridge when one comes to it (to)

_____

13)  step up to the plate (to)

_____

14)  sell oneself short (to)

_____

15)  discombobulated (to be)

_____

## 4.F ➜ More Writing Practice

**Task** ➜ Write a short passage using as many idioms as you can from this
lesson. The topic is your choice. Make it business-related if possible.

_____

_____

_____

_____

_____

_____

_____

_____

# Review #1

**Task** ➔ Fill in the blanks using the following.

| | | |
|---|---|---|
| 1. new blood | 10. rubberneck | 19. bend over backwards |
| 2. pull out all the stops | 11. bottom line | 20. in this neck of the woods |
| 3. schmooze | 12. in the market for | 21. bring in under budget |
| 4. hold | 13. have an in | 22. have kittens |
| 5. land | 14. the gist | 23. the icing on the cake |
| 6. throw cold water on | 15. go off the rails | 24. heavy hitter |
| 7. working lunch | 16. seal the deal | 25. ramp up |
| 8. think outside the box | 17. flesh out | 26. back-of-the-envelope calculations |
| 9. a happy camper | 18. beat the traffic | 27. stand to gain |

1.  The _____ is you need to _____ if
    you want to _____ .

2.  According to my _____ , we _____
    if we bring in _____ and _____ production.

3.  _____ , very few people are _____
    _____ a single-family home. Most want apartments or condos.

4.  Camille _____ a job with IBM because she _____ . Her
    boyfriend is a _____ in the finance department. _____
    _____ is she gets stock options.

5.  Daniela will not be _____ if you don't _____
    this project _____ .

6.  After Carolina _____ Hector's idea, he _____
    _____ . I'd avoid him. He's still _____ .

7.  A _____ is not the time to _____ .
    It is time to _____ the alcohol and _____ ideas.

8.  You often have to _____ when _____ .

9.  Tom gave Jill _____ of what happened during the meeting.

10. If you want to _____ , you'd better not _____ .

# Lesson #5 ➔ *All the Rage*

➔ **10:50 a.m.** Maria works at her desk. Beth enters.

**✳ ✳ ✳**

Beth:   Maria, I need you to fax this over to ABC Studios. It's the schedule for tomorrow's Uggs' shoot. Ms. Heatherspoon is going to be there, yes? She was on <u>the red-eye</u>, right?

Maria:  She booked into the Chelsea this morning. I confirmed it.

Beth:   Good. It's a relief to know the talent's <u>on board</u>. We <u>have a lot riding on this shoot</u>. *(sniffing)* What are you wearing?

Maria:  Don't you love it? It's *Passion Play* by Giorgio Klein. It's <u>all the rage</u>. The <u>tagline</u> is "Play with passion."

Beth:   Sounds pricey.

Maria:  Actually, it was <u>a freebie</u>. I got it at Macy's yesterday. It's causing a ton of buzz. People were lined up all around the block for it.

   *(Jake enters.)*

Jake:   I think Giorgio Klein is <u>spinning his wheels</u>. He used to be <u>a trendsetter</u>, but he hasn't hit one out of the park in ages. Personally, I think he's <u>resting on his laurels</u>. He needs <u>to face the music</u> and <u>pull the plug on his perfume line and his cookware</u>, and focus on his <u>core competency</u>: women's clothing.

Maria:  I beg to differ. Just because Giorgio Klein hasn't <u>sold out to Wal-Mart</u> doesn't mean he should rethink his business plan.

Beth:   For the record, I don't wear perfume. It gives me wicked migraines.

Jake:   <u>Ditto that</u>.

Maria:  Do you know what else is all the rage these days? Cookie butter. It's like peanut butter only instead of peanuts, it's crushed cashews and macadamias in milk chocolate. I spread it on everything. You want to try some? I brought a jar.

Jake:   Ah, no. That's <u>not my cup of tea</u>.

Beth:   Don't look at me. I put five pounds on just thinking about it.

   *(Beth and Jake exit talking.)*

## 5.A → Definitions

1) *red-eye (the)*
   - any midnight flight

2) *on board (to be)*
   - to be part of a plan

3) *have a lot riding on something/ someone (to)*
   - to depend greatly on

4) *all the rage (to be)*
   - to be fashionable/trendy/popular

5) *tagline (a)*
   - a slogan

6) *freebie (a)*
   - a free promotional gift

7) *spin one's wheels (to)*
   - to lack progress; to be stopped

8) *trendsetter (a)*
   - one who starts a trend

9) *rest on one's laurels (to)*
   - to depend on one's reputation with no further effort

10) *face the music (to)*
    - to face reality/the truth

11) *pull the plug (on) (to)*
    - to end a process

12) *core competency*
    - area of expertise; main skills

13) *sell out to someone/thing (to)*
    - to go against one's beliefs/policies for financial gain

14) *Ditto that.*
    - I agree. Me too. You can say that again.

15) *not my cup of tea (to be)*
    - not for me; not a preference

## 5.B → Practice

**Task** → Fill in the blanks using the idioms on the previous page.

1. Because that product was such a dog, the company decided _____ _____ and go back to the drawing board.

2. A _____ is someone who thinks outside the box.

3. Retailers in the U.S. _____ Black Friday.

4. The bottom line is we've been _____ for too long. It's time to step up to the plate and start thinking outside the box.

5. I know you like working here, but this company is going out of business. Believe me, it's time _____ and start pounding the pavement for a new job.

6. I prefer beer, thanks. Whiskey is _____ .

7. "That client talks out of both sides of his mouth," Hector said." _____", Maria replied.

8. A lot of famous people take _____ from L.A. to New York. If you take it, you never know with whom you might rub elbows.

9. When I bought my laptop, I told the clerk to hold the _____ . I've already got three printers. I don't need another.

10. Dave called to say he loved the idea. He is definitely _____ .

11. I take it you're working on the _____ for Biagi Pizza, yes?

12. Last year, stretchy jeans were _____ .

13. Michelle told Al to put a fire under it. He's been _____ for too long.

14. Apple is eating Microsoft's lunch. That said, Microsoft needs to face the music and focus more on their _____ : software.

15. I can't believe it. Lady Gaga _____ Disney!

## 5.C → The Story Continues

**Task** → Read the rest of the conversation, then answer the questions.

Beth:   So, Jake, how's it going?

Jake:   I have got a lot on my plate, but I'm managing to keep my head above water. Did you hear? My wife just had a baby.

Beth:   Congrats. Boy or girl?

Jake:   A boy. James Andrew.

Beth:   You must be so proud.

Jake:   Yeah. And bagged. He sleeps all day and cries all night. I have definitely hit the wall. How about you? What's shaking in your world?

Beth:   Nothing to write home about. Don't forget we have a working lunch. Mario Biagi is raising Cain.

Jake:   Again? What's wrong this time?

Beth:   That is the $64,000.00 question.*

## Questions

1. How many idioms can you identify in the passage above? What does each mean? Compare your choices to those on pg. 162. For definitions, see the word list, pg. 188.

2. What is the $64,000.00 question? Explain.

3. What is all the rage right now in your country and in the U.S.? Explain.

4. Many famous people have sold out. Do you think selling out is good or bad for one's image? Would you sell out? Explain.

5. Verbally summarize this lesson. Time yourself. You have 2 minutes.

* *See Movie-TV quotes pg. 214*

## 5.D → Expansion

**Task** → Match the expressions in column A with the definitions in column B.

**A**

1) black eye (a) ____

2) in the black (to be) ____

3) in the red (to be) ____

4) steal (a) ____

5) consumer traffic ____

6) complement (a) ____

7) compliant (to be) ____

8) strip mall (a) ____

9) big-box store (a) ____

10) locavore (a) ____

11) hypoallergenic ____

12) marketing mix ____

13) bull market (a) ____

14) bear market (a) ____

15) go on a shopping spree (to) ____

16) price fix (to) ____

17) go on a wild-goose chase (to) (S) ____

18) sleeper (a) ____

19) hard selling ____

20) soft selling ____

**B**

A) a person who supports local farmers

B) non allergenic

C) the four elements of a marketing plan: product, price, place, promotion; the 4Ps

D) the prolonged selling/holding of securities and commodities

E) to shop with no regard for cost

F) appealing to consumer needs and wants

G) a big retail store with low prices; Wal-Mart

H) to show a profit/gain

I) the high-volume trading of securities and commodities with prices rising

J) a mark of shame/failure

K) competitors agreeing to the same price

L) appealing to consumer greed, vanity, fear

M) the number of people moving through a retail area during business hours

N) a product of less value that sells with a main product, i.e., buns and hot dogs

O) to waste time searching in the wrong direction

P) a product with a low price; a bargain

Q) retail stores located near intersections

R) to follow the rules/law; to conform

S) a product that becomes a hit due to word-of-mouth advertising

T) to show a loss; in debt; negative

## 5.E ➜ Writing Practice

**Task** ➜ Write a sentence using each idiom.

1)   go on a shopping spree (to)

_____

2)   steal (a)

_____

3)   have a lot riding on something/someone (to)

_____

4)   all the rage (to be)

_____

5)   tagline (a)

_____

6)   freebie (a)

_____

7)   spin one's wheels (to)

_____

8)   trendsetter (a)

_____

9)   rest on one's laurels (to)

_____

10)  face the music (to)

_____

11)  pull the plug (on) (to)

_____

12)  core competency

_____

13)  in the red (to be)

_____

14)  in the black (to be)

_____

15)  not my cup of tea (to be)

_____

## 5.F ➜ More Writing Practice

**Task** ➜ Write a short passage using as many idioms as you can from this lesson. The topic is your choice. Make it business-related if possible.

_____

_____

_____

_____

_____

_____

_____

_____

# Lesson #6 ➜ *A Pink Slip*

➜ **11:10 a.m.** Joan and Judy discuss Chuck Cresten, an Austen account rep.

**✱ ✱ ✱**

Joan: He came in smelling of alcohol? Again?

Judy: Oh, yes. Not only that, but he's been <u>dipping into his expense account</u>. <u>Rumor has it that</u> he has a gambling problem, but don't quote me.

Joan: The man is a walking disaster.

Judy: He's been <u>moonlighting</u> for Art Advertising too.

Joan: What?

Judy: And I <u>caught him red-handed</u> stealing supplies from the storeroom.

Joan: I'd say it was <u>high time</u> Mr. Cresten <u>got his walking papers</u>.

Judy: I gave him <u>a pink slip</u> this morning.

Joan: And?

Judy: He <u>went ballistic</u>. He's threatening to sue us for <u>ageism</u>.

Joan: Ageism?

Judy And <u>drag Austen's name through the mud</u>.

Joan: Do you have a record of everything you've told me?

Judy: Yes. All on paper. And on the security cameras.

Joan: Good. Ageism my eye. If he takes us to court, he <u>won't have a leg to stand on</u>.

Judy: He did say that he'd be willing to negotiate a severance package.

Joan: I bet he did. Forget it. <u>Let the chips fall where they may</u>. I want him gone. Call security if you have to. We've <u>given him enough rope</u>.

Judy: That's what I like about you. You <u>take no prisoners</u>.

Joan: This is not personal. It's business.

Judy: You <u>took the words right out of my mouth</u>.

## 6.A ➔ Definitions

1) *dip into something (to)*
   - to steal from an account; to embezzle

2) *rumor has it (that)...*
   - the rumor is (that)...; the buzz is...

3) *moonlighting (to be)*
   - to be working off-hours tax free

4) *catch someone red-handed (to)*
   - to catch a person stealing

5) *high time*
   - about time; time to act

6) *get one's walking papers (to)*
   - to receive official notification of employment termination

7) *pink slip (a)*
   - a traditional official notice of employment termination

8) *go ballistic (to)*
   - to explode with sudden anger

9) *ageism*
   - age discrimination

10) *drag one's name through the mud (to)*
    - to attack one's reputation publicly

11) *have a leg to stand on (to not)*
    - to have no argument/defense

12) *let the chips fall where they may (to)*
    - to let destiny/fate decide

13) *have given one enough rope (to)*
    - to have given one enough time/ chances

14) *take no prisoners (to)*
    - to show no mercy; no compromise

15) *take the words right out of one's mouth (to)*
    - to say what another is thinking

## 6.B → Practice

**Task** → Fill in the blanks using the idioms on the previous page.

1.  If Rob gets stuck in traffic, he _____ .

2.  The accountant was arrested after he _____ a client's bank account.

3.  Don't quote me but _____ the president will be here next week.

4.  We have _____ Hal _____ , and look what happens.
    He's still asleep at the wheel.

5.  You _____ . I agree. It's time to clean house
    and bring in new blood.

6.  Racism, sexism and _____ are forms of work-place
    discrimination.

7.  I gave it my best shot trying to seal the deal. _____ .

8.  Carlos decided to pull the plug on _____ as a pizza driver. He felt
    he was just spinning his wheels while burning the candle at both ends.

9.  When I _____ Bob _____ stealing my sandwich in the
    lunchroom, he said he thought it was a freebie the client had sent over.

10. It's _____ we ran the numbers. We really need to see if our
    back-of-the envelope calculations are in the ball park or not.

11. After the president cheated on his wife, the press _____ .

12. I just _____ . That's okay. No big deal. Working
    for this company never was my cup of tea anyway.

13. You want to sue Apple for not offering enough phone apps? What do I think?
    To be honest, you _____ .

14. As we entered the meeting, Bob whispered, " _____ " .

15. Years ago, if you got _____ —a real pink piece of paper—you
    knew that your head was on the chopping block.

## 6.C ➜ The Story Continues

**Task** ➜ Read the rest of the conversation, then answer the questions.

Judy:     All right. So enough about Cresten. What about you? When was the last time you took a vacation?

Joan:     Vacation is not in my vocabulary.

Judy:     Joan, you need a break. You're running yourself ragged.

Joan:     I have a business to run. Besides, I'm that close to buying a place in Tribeca. A cozy-little pied-â-terre. All I have to do is sign on the dotted line, but I keep getting cold feet.

Judy      Why? Too much?

Joan:     No. The price is definitely doable. It's just that when people get older they usually retreat to the suburbs and don't come back. I am doing the exact opposite: going against the grain.

Judy:     Hey, if you like the place, go for it. Remember what you always tell me? Your motto? No regrets. What does Don think? Are you two moving in? Did his divorce papers come through?

Joan:     What is this? Twenty questions?

Judy:     Just asking. (*exiting*) He's definitely a keeper.

## Questions

1.  How many idioms can you identify in the passage above? What does each mean? Compare your choices to those on pg. 163. For definitions, see the word list, pg. 188.

2.  Is ageism a problem in your country? What about sexism? Explain.

3.  In your country, how does an employee receive a notice of job termination? What is the procedure? Explain.

4.  Why is Joan reluctant to take a vacation? What would you do? Explain.

5.  Verbally summarize this lesson. Time yourself. You have <u>2</u> minutes.

# 6.D → Expansion

**Task** → Match the expressions in column A with the definitions in column B.

| | A | | B |
|---|---|---|---|
| 1) | ameliorate (to) ____ | A) | rarely |
| 2) | man up (to) ____ | B) | to act like a man; be brave/strong |
| 3) | open a can of worms (to) ____ | C) | to make better; to improve |
| 4) | double-down (to) ____ | D) | reduction in force; to be laid off to reduce the number of employees due to a lack of work/money/reorganization, etc. |
| 5) | wash-out (a) ____ | | |
| 6) | RIFed (to be) ____ | E) | a failure; a disappointment |
| 7) | get the axe (to) ____ | F) | to double one's bet; to work twice as hard; to be more committed |
| 8) | let sleeping dogs lie (to) (S) ____ | | |
| 9) | need something like one needs a hole in the head (to) ____ | G) | to be fired |
| | | H) | to leave alone to avoid trouble |
| 10) | dirty laundry ____ | I) | a big and unexpected surprise |
| 11) | cruel to be kind (to be) (S) ____ | J) | embarrassing private business that becomes public |
| 12) | daycation (a) ____ | | |
| 13) | suffer fools lightly (to not) ____ | K) | a day trip |
| 14) | golden parachute (a) ____ | L) | to have neither need nor desire for |
| 15) | bombshell (a) ____ | M) | a well-funded retirement plan |
| 16) | gender neutral (to be) ____ | N) | to cause pain for a beneficial effect |
| 17) | once in a blue moon ____ | O) | to create more problems while trying to solve one problem |
| 18) | nevertiree (a) ____ | | |
| 19) | staycation (a) ____ | P) | to favor neither sex; equal |
| 20) | straw that broke the camel's back (the) ____ | Q) | the last act in a series of unacceptable acts |
| | | R) | one who will never retire |
| | | S) | to have no patience for stupidity |
| | | T) | a stay-at-home vacation |

## 6.E ➜ Writing Practice

**Task** ➜ Write a sentence using each idiom.

1)    double-down (to)

_____

2)    rumor has it that...

_____

3)    open a can of worms (to)

_____

4)    catch someone red-handed (to)

_____

5)    high time

_____

6)    pink slip (a)

_____

7)    once in a blue moon

_____

8)    go ballistic (to)

_____

9)    ageism

_____

10)   drag one's name through the mud (to)

_____

11)   have a leg to stand on (to not)

_____

12)   let the chips fall where they may (to)

_____

13)   cruel to be kind (to be)

_____

14)   take no prisoners (to)

_____

15)   take the words right out of one's mouth (to)

_____


## 6.F ➜ More Writing Practice

**Task** ➜ Write a short passage using as many idioms as you can from this
lesson. The topic is your choice. Make it business-related if possible.

_____

_____

_____

_____

_____

_____

_____

_____

# <u>Lesson #7</u> ➔ *The Only Game in Town*

➔ **11:00 a.m.** Talita Alves enters Austen Advertising. She approaches Maria.

**✻ ✻ ✻**

<u>Talita</u>: Hi. Is Ms. Austen in?

<u>Maria</u>: I'm sorry. Ms. Austen is <u>tied up</u> at the moment. Can I help you?

<u>Talita</u>: I'm a third-year student at the Architecture Institute. I'm looking for a summer internship. Does Austen Advertising offer any?

<u>Maria</u>: We do. Do you have a résumé?

<u>Talita</u>: Yes. Here it is. Last summer I interned for Paul Holmes. Do you know him? He designed the MET extension. I also interned for Linda Evans, the industrial designer. She's <u>a kick</u>, and totally <u>off her rocker</u>. By the way, does Joey Bostick still work here?

<u>Maria</u>: He does.

<u>Talita</u>: Tell him Talita says hi.

<u>Maria</u>: I'll do that. Tell me, Ms. Alves, do you have any experience working in an ad agency?

<u>Talita</u>: No. But I'm willing to learn. I'll do anything: make coffee, take out the garbage. Please, I just want <u>to get my foot in the door</u>.

<u>Maria</u>: Advertising is <u>a far cry from architecture</u>.

<u>Talita</u>: I know. My mom wants me <u>to follow in her footsteps</u>, but to be honest, I'm not <u>cut out to be an architect</u>. It's not where I want <u>to hang my hat</u>.

<u>Maria</u>: Have you tried other ad agencies?

<u>Talita</u>: No. You're <u>the only game in town</u>. Serious. No one can <u>hold a candle to you guys</u>, not even the big agencies. I would <u>kill to work here</u>. Really. Can I leave my portfolio? It shows my <u>skill set</u>. I don't want <u>to blow my own horn</u>, but I'm <u>a wiz at Photoshop</u>.

<u>Maria</u>: Your résumé <u>will suffice</u> for now, thanks. If you get a call, bring your portfolio then. Anything else?

<u>Talita</u>: Nope. That's it. Say hello to Alberto Pena for me too. We went to high school together. Bye.

*(As Talita exits, Hector enters.)*

## 7.A → Definitions

1) *tied up (to be)*
   - to be busy/not available

   _____

2) *kick (to be a)*
   - to be fun/great/a blast

   _____

3) *off one's rocker (to be)*
   - to be crazy/eccentric/unpredictable

   _____

4) *get one's foot in the door (to)*
   - to gain entry into a chosen place

   _____

5) *far cry from (to be a)*
   - to be very different from

   _____

6) *follow in one's footsteps (to)*
   - to do the same as one's parent

   _____

7) *cut out to be something/someone (to be)*
   - to feel born to do; to be destined

   _____

8) *hang one's hat (to)*
   - to take up residence; to be part of

   _____

9) *the only game in town*
   - the only/best choice

   _____

10) *no one can hold a candle to someone/something*
    - no competition; no equal

   _____

11) *kill to do something/be someone (to)*
    - to do anything to attain/become

   _____

12) *skill set*
    - one's abilities/talents/expertise

   _____

13) *blow one's (own) horn (to)*
    - to brag/boast; to self promote

   _____

14) *wiz at something (to be a)*
    - to be a wizard; one with special talent

   _____

15) *suffice (to)*
    - to satisfy; to be enough

   _____

## 7.B → Practice

**Task** → Fill in the blanks using the idioms on the previous page.

1. Sally loves movies. She would _____ to work in Hollywood.

2. Harold is _____ fixing computers.

3. If you want to swim with the sharks, you can't be afraid _____
_____ .

4. Sylvia had to cancel the working lunch because she was all _____ .

5. Your _____ describes your core competency.

6. When Charlie wheels and deals, he takes no prisoners. If you didn't know
him, you would say he was _____ .

7. In this neck of the woods, there are a lot of big box stores. But for price and
value, Wal-Mart is really _____ .

8. Nigel tried to fix his car, but in the end he had to admit that he was not _____
_____ a mechanic.

9. Moonlighting is _____ having a career.

10. Sara _____ her mother's _____ and became
a dentist.

11. When you fly internationally, the only document that will _____
for personal I.D. is a valid passport.

12. When Mariana retires, she wants _____ in Florida.

13. After applying to Goldman Sachs for many years, Berta finally _____
_____ .

14. As far as Tim is concerned, _____ Google.

15. I've never met Paul, but rumor has it he's _____ .

## 7.C ➜ The Story Continues

**Task** ➜ Read the rest of the conversation, then answer the questions.

Hector:   Who was that all bright-eyed and bushy-tailed?

Maria:   An intern applicant. She's quite the name-dropper.

Hector:   It's not what you know, but who you know, right?

Maria:   That's how you got this job.

Hector:   Okay, don't rub it in.

Maria:   And you still owe me. So when are you taking me out for dinner?

Hector:   Where do you want to go?

Maria:   How about that new French restaurant, La Baguette?

Hector:   That place? Forget it. It costs an arm and a leg. Besides, you practically have to inherit a reservation. How about pizza? Pizza, a couple of brewskies and the Yanks on TV. Oh, yeah. Now we're talking.

Maria:   You know what I like about you, Hector Gomez?

Hector:   What?

Maria:   *(exiting)* You know how to treat a girl right.

## Questions

1. How many idioms can you identify in the passage above? What does each mean? Compare your choices to those on pg. 165. For definitions, see the word list, pg. 188.

2. Talita is very American when she enters Austen Advertising and starts asking for Joan Austen and about intern and employment opportunities without an appointment. Would you do the same in your country? Explain.

3. In your country, when applying for an internship and/or a job, what is the process? What about in the U.S.? Explain.

4. Why does Maria want Hector to take her out? Explain.

5. Verbally summarize this lesson. Time yourself. You have 2 minutes.

## 7.D → Expansion

**Task** → Match the expressions in column A with the definitions in column B.

**A**

1) cold call (to) ____

2) the green-eyed monster (S) ____

3) old hand at something (to be an) ____

4) blow something (to) ____

5) tyro (a) ____

6) braggart (a) ____

7) blowback ____

8) green around the gills (to be) ___

9) killer instinct ____

10) kick off (to) ____

11) at a crossroads (to be) ____

12) dressed to kill (to be) ____

13) killer app (a) ____

14) at the top of one's game (to be) ____

15) hit the reset button (to) ____

16) mettle ____

17) glib (to be) ____

18) headhunter (a) ____

19) laundry list (a) ____

20) push-over (to be a) ____

**B**

A) to make a big mistake; to screw up

B) one who always blows his/her horn

C) an unexpected/unwanted effect

D) to be performing one's best

E) to be facing a difficult choice

F) to start

G) to go back to the drawing board

H) strength of character; will

I) to be superficial; lacking depth

J) jealousy

K) a to-do list

L) a computer application (software) that makes a computer worth owning

M) to be dressed for success

N) a ruthless desire to succeed/win

O) to sell/pitch something by phone

P) to have a lot of experience doing something

Q) a job recruiter

R) one who is easily persuaded

S) a beginner/newbie/neophyte

T) to lack experience; a tyro

## 8.B ➜ Practice

**Task** ➜ Fill in the blanks using the idioms on the previous page.

1.  To avoid the high cost of maintaining large _____ , many publishers, large and small, are now print-on-demand (POD) only.

2.  _____ is not my cup of tea. Thanks, anyway.

3.  We've been spinning our wheels for too long. It is time _____ _____ and get to work. We have a lot riding on this product.

4.  _____ . In this business, we take no prisoners.

5.  _____ this year is a far cry from what it was last year. I suggest you run the numbers again just to double check.

6.  Dave is so wishy-washy. For once, I wish he'd just _____ .

7.  I don't know why the media is dragging his name through the mud. Don't they _____ ?

8.  Toni is really _____ the money moonlighting as an estate planner.

9.  Sorry, but you don't really have the skill set to be a TV _____ .

10. Why did I go ballistic? Because that fender-bender _____ five G's. I am not a happy camper, believe me.

11. We need to ramp up production. The orders are just _____ .

12. My assignment is only for six months, so I'm not in the market for an unfurnished apartment. I need _____ ASAP.

13. Bob Catelin is not one to blow his own horn. Case in point: he thinks Bobcat Beer is _____ . I beg to differ. I think the sky is the limit.

14. Do you know what the _____ are for the Upper East Side of Manhattan?

15. We need to face the music. _____ has failed to increase our bottom line. It's time to throw cold water on that idea.

## 8.C ➜ The Story Continues

**Task** ➜ Read the rest of the conversation, then answer the questions.

Steve:   Just between me and you, Mr. Catelin, Brad Clooney drinks Bobcat beer. And get this: he's got a bar in his Hollywood basement. This old English pub.

Bob:   Well, I'll be.

Steve:   Not only that, but he's got Bobcat Beer on tap. After a long day of making movies, he goes down to his own private pub and pours himself a cold Bobcat.

Bob:   No fooling.

Steve:   Well? Should I give Mr. Clooney a call? Just say the word.

Bob:   I don't know. This is a tough call. I'm of two minds. Bobcat's always been a family business but at the end of the day, making money's the name of the game. Any businessman worth his salt knows that. And to do that, to make money, Bobcat's got to go national, no ifs, ands or buts. We've got to roll with the punches and run with the big boys.

Steve:   Look, why don't you sleep on it. Okay? I'll touch base with you tomorrow and we can go from there.

Bob:   Sounds like a plan. Now how about that beer?

## Questions

1. How many idioms can you identify in the passage above? What does each mean? Compare your choices to those on pg. 166. For definitions, see the word list, pg. 188.

2. Do you think Steve's pitch is persuasive? Why? Why not? Explain.

3. In the end, what does Bob Catelin decide to do? What would you do? Explain.

4. Organic products are all the rage in the U.S. Why? What about in your country? Explain.

5. Verbally summarize this lesson. Time yourself. You have <u>2</u> minutes.

## 8.D → Expansion

**Task** → Match the expressions in column A with the definitions in column B.

**A**

1) take a crack at something (to) ____

2) track record ____

3) on track (to be) ____

4) To thine own self be true. (S) ____

5) pitch (to) ____

6) when pigs fly ____

7) when the chips are down ____

8) greentail (to) ____

9) the nitty-gritty ____

10) run a tight ship (to) ____

11) abandon ship (to) ____

12) plug (to) ____

13) chug along (to) ____

14) weigh in on something (to) ____

15) give one the run-around (to) ____

16) letter-of-intent (a) (LOI) ____

17) boilerplate (to be) ____

18) drum up business (to) ____

19) dyed-in-the wool (to be) ____

20) pull the wool over one's eyes (to) ___

**B**

A) to deliver a brief argument aimed at selling an idea/product

B) the details/basic facts

C) to pitch a product/idea; to advertise

D) Take care of yourself first.

E) to move at a constant speed

F) to be moving in the right direction on time

G) to try and generate business

H) to attempt/try

I) to manage efficiently; disciplined

J) to throw in the towel

K) standard legal language/legalese

L) to delay/avoid/frustrate

M) to give one's opinion

N) to sell eco-friendly products

O) to fool/deceive someone

P) when one feels defeated; when one is at a low point

Q) a history of past performance

R) to be a true believer; unchangeable

S) impossible; unlikely

T) a letter outlining an agreement between two parties before they seal the deal

## 8.E ➜ Writing Practice

**Task** ➜ Write a sentence using each idiom.

1)  Joe (a cup of)

_____

2)  revenue

_____

3)  lay one's cards on the table (to)

_____

4)  word-of-mouth advertising

_____

5)  pile up (to)

_____

6)  inventory

_____

7)  demographic(s)

_____

8)  rake something in (to)

_____

9)  pitchman (a)

_____

10)  set one back (to)

_____

11) roll up one's sleeves (to)

_____

12) small potatoes (to be)

_____

13) have bigger fish to fry (to)

_____

14) lay it on the line (to)

_____

15) the total package

_____

## 8.F ➔ More Writing Practice

**Task** ➔ Write a short passage using as many idioms as you can from this lesson. The topic is your choice. Make it business-related if possible.

_____

_____

_____

_____

_____

_____

_____

_____

## Review #2

**Task** ➜ Fill in the blanks using the following.

| | | |
|---|---|---|
| 1. face the music | 10. set one back | 19. get one's foot in the door |
| 2. inventory | 11. in the red | 20. have bigger fish to fry |
| 3. demographics | 12. the red-eye | 21. let me lay it on the line |
| 4. the total package | 13. Joe | 22. no one can hold a candle to |
| 5. no ifs, ands or buts | 14. kick | 23. the only game in town |
| 6. pile up | 15. walking papers | 24. spin one's wheels |
| 7. a wiz at | 16. pitchman | 25. raking it in |
| 8. high time | 17. a far cry from | 26. hang one's hat |
| 9. small potatoes | 18. a freebie | 27. blow one's own horn |

1. In this dog-eat-dog world, if you want to _____ ,
   you really have to _____ , _____ .

2. We have to _____ , people. Sales are _____
   what they were last year. I think we need to give Brad Clooney his _____
   _____ and find a new _____ .

3. In this neck of the woods, office space will _____ two grand a
   square foot. _____ , really, compared to what's out there.

4. Our _____ is _____ . It's definitely
   going to put us _____ . What we need is a cash cow.

5. You won't believe whom I sat beside on _____ . Brad Clooney!
   The guy's a real _____ . Rumor has it he's _____ .

6. Stop worrying about when you'll get your new laptop. You _____
   _____ , like researching the _____ for Boston.

7. _____ . It's _____ we started thinking
   outside the box. If not, we will continue to _____ .

8. _____ Patricia. She is _____ .

9. I want to _____ here because it's _____ . By
   the way, I'm _____ Illustrator and I make a great cup of _____ .

10. There is a big difference between _____ and a free ride.

# Lesson #9 ➜ *The Working Lunch*

➜ **11:45 a.m.** Beth enters the conference room.

✳ ✳ ✳

Beth: Okay, people, let's <u>buckle down</u>. We need to put our heads together and <u>work this thing through</u>. Failure is not an option.* We are <u>under the gun</u> and Mr. Pizza is waiting.

Rick: Why did Biagi <u>pan the last idea</u>? <u>Run that by me again</u>.

Beth: He didn't like the idea of an elephant making pizza. He thought it was, and I quote, "<u>Half-baked</u>."

Debra: Where's Joan? I'd thought she'd be here.

Beth: She can't make it. She's schmoozing with <u>a suit</u> from Eagle Securities. She did, however, leave me our <u>marching orders</u>: "Make Mr. Pizza happy." Okay, people, <u>the clock is running</u>. Rick, you want to jump in here?

Rick: I like the elephant.

Beth: <u>Water under the bridge</u>. Proceed.

Rick: Right. So picture this. A young man drags himself through a desert. He's <u>at the end of his rope</u>. He comes to a crossroads. He sees a parked car. The driver is eating a Biagi pizza. Beside the pizza on the car is a big bottle of cold water. The dying man looks at the water, the pizza, the water, then...

Beth: He grabs a slice of pizza and he's <u>right as rain</u>.

Rick: Bingo. Well?

Judy: I like it. The <u>twist</u> is good. Drives the point home. Beth?

Beth: I'm sold. But that's me. Biagi is <u>a whole different story</u>. Debra? You're up.

Debra: Okay, so this is the scene. A happy family is eating dinner around a nice cozy kitchen table. Everyone is <u>scarfing down Biagi pizza</u>. Dad, two kids, baby, grandma, the dog. <u>You know the drill</u>. Total Rockwell.**

Beth: Okay, so where's mom?

*\* See Movie-TV quotes pg. 214*
*\*\* Norman Rockwell, American genre painter (1894-1978)*

## 9.A → Definitions

1) *buckle down (to)*
   - to get serious and work

2) *work something through (to)*
   - to find a solution to a problem

3) *under the gun (to be)*
   - to be under great pressure

4) *pan something (to)*
   - to reject with severe criticism

5) *Run that by me again.*
   - Please tell me again.

6) *half-baked (to be)*
   - not complete; not serious or thought through

7) *suit (a)*
   - a businessperson

8) *marching orders*
   - instructions from a superior

9) *clock is running (the)*
   - the deadline is approaching

10) *water under the bridge*
    - a past event that cannot be revisited; What's done is done. (S)

11) *at the end of one's rope (to be)*
    - to have run out of patience/options

12) *twist (a)*
    - an expected/surprise ending to a story/movie/event, etc.

13) *whole different story (to be a)*
    - to be completely different

14) *scarf down (to)*
    - to eat with great appetite; to wolf down

15) *You know the drill.*
    - You know what to do; you get the picture.

## 9.B → Practice

**Task** → Fill in the blanks using the idioms on the previous page.

1.  We were about to seal the deal when the client _____ it completely.

2.  Rethinking that slogan is a waste of time. It's _____ . Besides, we have bigger fish to fry.

3.  Revenue was up how much last quarter? _____ .

4.  Sorry, but putting chocolate on a pizza is _____ idea.

5.  We just got our _____ . It's time to roll up our sleeves and go to work.

6.  Bernie's been burning the midnight oil trying to make the client happy, yet he's just spinning his wheels. Believe me, he's _____ .

7.  Don't you just love _____ at the end of that movie?

8.  Amy, when you're finished running the numbers, send them out to each partner, okay? _____ .

9.  John was so hungry, he _____ all the donuts.

10. Pete, are you on board? We've got to know. _____ .

11. Charles is _____ . Everyone expects him to follow in his father's footsteps and take over the family business, but Charles is a far cry from his father. All Charles does is waffle.

12. No. Manhattan is not like Los Angeles. Los Angeles is _____ _____ .

13. Even though the problem is small potatoes, you still have to _____ _____ .

14. If you want to keep your job, you really have _____ and hit one out of the park or else your head will be on the chopping block.

15. That restaurant looks expensive. It is full of _____ .

## 9.C ➔ The Story Continues

**Task** ➔ Read the rest of the conversation, then answer the questions.

Debra: Mom walks in all smiles and says, "Who wants dessert?" Everyone is surprised. Why? Because mom is holding an apple pie, a chocolate cake? No. It gets better. She's got another piping-hot Biagi pizza. The happy family cheers and digs in. They just can't get enough.

Rick: Pizza for dessert? I'll get back to you on that one.

Debra: It's not dessert. It's Biagi pizza. It's better than dessert. Hey, that can be our tagline: Biagi Pizza. Better than dessert.

Rick: Like I said, I'll get back to you.

Debra: I beg to differ. It touches all bases. Tradition. Family. Home. Pets. Beth? Correct me if I'm wrong, but that's what Biagi wants. Pure MOR Right?

Beth: You got it. Okay, people, so we have desert pizza and pizza for dessert. Let's flesh out a few more ideas before we nail this thing down.

## Questions

1. How many idioms can you identify in the passage above? What does each mean? Compare your choices to those on pg. 168. For definitions, see the word list, pg. 188.

2. Which of the two commercial ideas do you prefer? Why? Explain.

3. Norman Rockwell's paintings show traditional American families with strong family values. Are those values the same or are they changing in the U.S.? What about in your country? Explain.

4. What will Beth and everyone do next ? Why? Explain.

5. Verbally summarize this lesson. Time yourself. You have <u>2</u> minutes.

## 9.D → Expansion

**Task** → Match the expressions in column A with the definitions in column B.

**A**

**B**

1) knock one's socks off (to) ____

2) water down (to) ____

3) hold water (to not) ____

4) dead in the water (to be) ____

5) mouthwatering (to be) ____

6) watering hole (a) ____

7) bail out of (to) ____

8) bailout (to) ____

9) hit-and-miss (to be) ____

10) in too deep (to be) ____

11) burn one's bridges (to) ____

12) bridge the gap (to) ____

13) steal a march on (to) ____

14) whole different kettle of fish (to be a) ____

15) stick to one's guns (to) ____

16) smoking gun (a) ____

17) gun for (to) ____

18) big guns (the) ____

19) hired gun (a) ____

20) To be or not to be, that is the question. (S) ____

A) to lack persuasiveness

B) to look delicious/appetizing

C) to be too involved to exit without a loss

D) to make a decision that will have negative consequences resulting in a loss of personal/business connections

E) to go after with determination

F) to make a connection between opposites

G) to arrive before another; to gain the advantage due to a quick first move

H) to hold one's position; to refuse to budge

I) evidence of a crime/guilt

J) heavy hitters; A-players; the big dogs

K) to impress greatly; to amaze

L) to exit from

M) to be stopped; no progress

N) to reduce in strength

O) a specialist brought in to fix a problem

P) to rescue with financial help

Q) To do it or not. That is the $64,000.00 question.

R) a restaurant/bar one visits regularly

S) to be irregular in quality/outcome

T) a whole different story

## 9.E ➜ **Writing Practice**

**Task** ➜ Write a sentence using each idiom.

1) buckle down (to)

_____

2) work something through (to)

_____

3) under the gun (to be)

_____

4) pan (to)

_____

5) whole different kettle of fish (to be a)

_____

6) half-baked (to be)

_____

7) stick to one's guns (to)

_____

8) marching orders

_____

9) clock is running (the)

_____

10) water under the bridge (to be)

_____

11)   at the end of one's rope (to be)

_____

12)   knock one's socks off (to)

_____

13)   mouthwatering (to be)

_____

14)   scarf down (to)

_____

15)   in too deep (to be)

_____


## 9.F ➜ More Writing Practice

**Task** ➜ Write a short passage using as many idioms as you can from this
lesson. The topic is your choice. Make it business-related if possible.

_____

_____

_____

_____

_____

_____

_____

_____

_____

# Lesson #10 ➜ *The Power Lunch*

➜ **12:15 p.m.** Joan dines with Diana Atkinson at the *21 Club.* Ms. Atkinson is the CEO of *Eagle Securities*, a top Wall Street securities company.

✳ ✳ ✳

Diana: As you know, our business has traditionally been institutional investors. However, we want <u>to branch out into individual investors</u>. Before we do, however, we want to test the waters first.

Joan: So how can Austen help?

Diana: What do you think of Eagle's image? And <u>don't mince words</u>.

Joan: Personally, I think your image needs <u>an overhaul</u>. You really need to rethink it if you want <u>to crack the individual investor market</u>.

Diana: Really? But <u>why mess with success</u>?

Joan: Because your logo hasn't changed since 1910.

Diana: Changing the logo would be a tough call. The board is still <u>an old boys' club</u>. Change is not in their vocabulary.

Joan: You don't have to change the logo, <u>per se</u>. Just bring it up to date. Also, the average investor doesn't wear pin stripes. She's a suburban soccer mom. She's got a husband, an SUV, a couple of kids and a dog. To reach her, you have <u>to speak her language</u>. Wall Street is a far cry from Main Street, especially in this economy with everyone <u>pinching pennies</u>.

Diana: So if we give you <u>the green light</u>, how would we proceed?

Joan: I'd <u>set you up with Jane Frost</u>. She's our top account executive. She'll work out a business plan based on your needs, everything <u>from soup to nuts</u>.

Diana: I will need <u>to get buy-in from the board first</u>. I'll let you know. But we are definitely <u>on the same page</u> about the image overhaul.

Joan: Great. Here, let me get the bill.

Diana: Thanks. So how's your stock portfolio?

Joan: Speaking of which, I need some advice.

Diana: I'm <u>all ears</u>.

## 10.A → Definitions

1) *branch out into something (to)*
   - to expand into; to diversify

2) *mince words (to)*
   - to avoid the truth

3) *overhaul (an)*
   - a rebuilding/redesigning to improve

4) *crack something (to)*
   - to enter a market, etc.

5) *Why mess with success?*
   - Why change a winning game plan?

6) *old boys' clubs (an)*
   - a traditional club only men can join

7) *per se*
   - in and of itself

8) *speak one's language (to)*
   - to communicate using the vocabulary
   of one's audience/market

9) *pinch pennies (to)*
   - to live frugally; to control costs by
   limiting expenses

10) *green light (the)*
   - the OK; the go-ahead; permission

11) *set one up with someone (to)*
   - to arrange to have a meeting with
   someone

12) *from soup to nuts*
   - controlling a process from start
   to finish

13) *get buy-in (from someone) (to)*
   - to get support/agreement

14) *on the same page (to be)*
   - to be in agreement; to see eye to eye

15) *all ears (to be)*
   - to be listening closely

## 10.B ➜ Practice

**Task** ➜ Fill in the blanks using the idioms on the previous page.

1. Many in America believe that the tax laws should be _____ .

2. In this neck of the woods, if you want _____ the coffee-shop market, you really have to think outside the box.

3. If you seal the deal, that means everyone is _____ .

4. That hotel was great. They took care of everything, _____ .

5. What I admire about Joan is that she thinks outside the box and she takes no prisoners. She definitely _____ .

6. The bottom line is we need to start _____ or else we will end up in the red.

7. Joan will give this project _____ only if we bring it in under budget.

8. Lidia jumped ship because her old company was _____ and she was just spinning her wheels.

9. I'm not going _____ . We need to clean house and bring in new blood.

10. Joe thinks we should _____ the donut business. Personally, I think he's off his rocker. Dunkin Donuts will eat our lunch.

11. The slogan _____ is fine. You just have to flesh out some better ideas for the logo. And remember: the clock is running.

12. _____ ? Because we've been resting on our laurels for too long. We have to put a fire under it and step up the plate.

13. Bob thought the board would pan his idea, but he _____ instead. He is definitely a happy camper. Look at him. He looks like the cat that ate the canary.

14. Howard and Sally did what? Tell me. I'm _____ .

15. Maria _____ Joan _____ Abby Finestein, the best real estate agent in Manhattan.

## 10.C ➜ The Story Continues

**Task** ➜ Read the rest of the conversation, then answer the questions.

Joan:    I'm going to buy a place in the city. Nothing fancy, just a simple pied-à-terre.

Diana:   A simple pied-à-terre will cost you an arm and a leg—and then some.

Joan:    I know. That's why I'm going to sell some stock. Do you think I should unload Apple or just sit on it?

Diana:   I'd hold on to it. Apple's product pipeline is unsurpassed. I would, however, unload Microsoft. They've been spinning their wheels for years. Also, I've heard that the new Windows is being trashed by beta testers. That doesn't augur well for Mr. Gates.

Joan:    What about Amazon? Buy, sell, or hold?

Diana:   Buy it and hold it. Absolutely. Amazon is the biggest online retailer. Nobody even comes close. In ten years, you will double your money.

Joan:    What about commission? Is it still seven percent?

Diana:   Tell you what. Show me some logo designs and we'll talk about the commission. In the meantime, I've got to skedaddle. Call me. And say hello to Don for me. Let me know when you're going to tie the knot.

## Questions

1. How many idioms can you identify? What does each mean in this context? Compare your choices to those on pg. 169. For definitions, see the word list, pg. 188.

2. Which stock do you think Joan will sell? Why? Explain.

3. In the U.S., many companies are still old boys' clubs. What about in your country? Explain.

4. What does Joan mean when she says, "Wall Street is a far cry from Main Street?" Explain.

5. Verbally summarize this lesson. Time yourself. You have 2 minutes.

## 10.D → Expansion

**Task** → Match the expressions in column A with the definitions in column B.

**A**

1)  face time ____

2)  give feedback (to) ____

3)  rearrange the deck chairs on the Titanic (to) ____

4)  straight shooter (a) ____

5)  Shoot. ____

6)  make short shrift of (to) (S) ____

7)  white collar ____

8)  blue collar ____

9)  fall through the cracks (to) ____

10) hit the glass ceiling (to) ____

11) up the ante (to) ____

12) before the bell ____

13) after the bell ____

14) portfolio (a) ____

15) asset (an) ____

16) put into layman's language (to) ____

17) fungible (to be) ____

18) paradigm shift (a) ____

19) feel the pinch (to) ____

20) bad penny (a) ____

**B**

A)  one who is honest/frank

B)  to explain in simple (non expert) English

C)  a group of financial investments

D)  labor

E)  to feel the effects of cost cutting

F)  to hit an invisible barrier that stops advancement due to being female

G)  a change in basic assumptions

H)  doing business face-to-face

I)  to try and reform a failing system

J)  management

K)  to be interchangeable/substitutable

L)  Go ahead. I'm all ears.

M)  a person with a bad reputation

N)  before the New York Stock Exchange (NYSE) opens at 9:30 a.m.

O)  a thing of value that creates income

P)  to do away with quickly

Q)  to give constructive criticism

R)  to take on more risk by increasing a bet; to increase the pressure

S)  to go by unnoticed only to become an issue later on

T)  after the New York Stock Exchange (NYSE) closes at 4:00 p.m.

## 10.E ➜ Writing Practice

**Task** ➜ Write a sentence using each idiom.

1)  branch out into something (to)

_____

2)  mince words (to)

_____

3)  straight shooter (a)

_____

4)  crack something (to)

_____

5)  bad penny (a)

_____

6)  old boys' club (an)

_____

7)  per se

_____

8)  speak one's language (to)

_____

9)  pinch pennies (to)

_____

10)  green light (the)

_____

11) set one up with someone (to)

_____

12) from soup to nuts

_____

13) give feedback (to)

_____

14) on the same page (to be)

_____

15) hit the glass ceiling (to)

_____

## 10.F ➜ More Writing Practice

**Task** ➜ Write a short passage using as many idioms as you can from this lesson. The topic is your choice. Make it business-related if possible.

_____

_____

_____

_____

_____

_____

_____

_____

# Lesson #11 ➜ *Mum's the Word*

➜ **2:00 p.m.** Judy enters Joan's office.

**✽ ✽ ✽**

Judy: So how was lunch?

Joan: Eagle Securities wants <u>a make-over</u>. They're branching out into individual investors but are afraid their <u>stodgy</u> image won't <u>fly</u> in suburbia.

Judy: So no deal?

Joan: No deal yet. But <u>when push comes to shove</u>, it's ours. How was the meeting?

Judy: We brainstormed over pizza. Rick and Debra have definitely <u>nailed it</u>.

Joan: That's what you said the last time. I hate <u>to sound like a broken record</u>, but if we don't <u>come through</u> this time, Mr. Pizza might pull the plug.

Judy: I think we're finally on the right track. You watch. Before the week is out, we'll have Mario Biagi <u>eating out of our hands</u>.

Joan: Let's not <u>count our chickens before they're hatched</u>, okay?

Judy: Right. So what did you want to see me about?

Joan: After lunch, I checked out office space up on Madison.

Judy: Madison Avenue? Are you serious? What was the PSF?

Joan: One thousand. Three-thousand square feet should do us.

Judy: Ah, I don't want <u>to burst your bubble</u>, but that is a little <u>out of our league</u>. Maybe we should <u>set our sights a little lower</u>.

Joan: Revenues are up, yes?

Judy: They are. Still, Madison Avenue?

Joan: In this business, <u>you don't get a second chance to make a first</u> impression. And it all starts with the right address. In other words, we have to spend money to make money.

Judy: It sounds like you've already sealed the deal.

Joan: I have. Here's the lease. Please <u>go over it with a fine-tooth comb</u>. I'm sure it's pretty much boilerplate. Still, I don't want any surprises <u>at the eleventh hour</u>.

## 11.A → Definitions

1) *make-over (a)*
   - a change of image; a new look

2) *stodgy (to be)*
   - to be old-fashioned/conservative

3) *fly (to)*
   - to succeed

4) *when push comes to shove*
   - when words become action

5) *nail something (to)*
   - to get it right; to succeed

6) *sound like a broken record (to)*
   - to repeat again and again

7) *come through (to)*
   - to perform as expected; to succeed

8) *eat out of one's hand (to)*
   - to control/persuade easily

9) *count one's chickens before they are hatched (to not)*
   - to warn against assuming a gain before it is realized

11) *burst one's bubble (to)*
   - to wake one up to reality

10) *out of one's league (to be)*
   - to be beyond one's reach/ability

12) *set one's sights a little lower/ higher (to)*
   - to reduce/increase expectations based on one's abilities/resources, etc.

13) *You don't get a second chance to make a first impression.*
   - You get one chance to succeed.

14) *go over with a fine-tooth comb (to)*
   - to inspect carefully

15) *at the eleventh hour*
   - at the last minute/second

## 11.B → Practice

**Task** →Fill in the blanks using the idioms on the previous page.

1.  Ali hopes his new invention will _____ in the American market.

2.  _____ , I will be there in a New-York minute.

3.  I hate _____ , but the sky is the limit.

4.  Joan really _____ when she threw cold water on my idea.

5.  If you don't _____ your quarterly report _____ _____ , the CFO will have kittens if she finds a mistake.

6.  We thought our jobs were safe, but _____ , we all got pink slips. Suffice it to say, we are not happy campers.

7.  Becoming president of the United States is a little _____ .

8.  Remember what I said. If you don't _____ , you will have to face the music. You've been resting on your laurels for too long.

9.  _____ . We still need to get buy-in from the CEO. If not, we'll just be spinning our wheels.

10. The first rule of business: _____ .

11. I love the new business plan. You really _____ it, everything from soup to nuts.

12. I agree. Our corporate image is quite _____ , but why mess with success?

13. If you want to be a heavy hitter, you really need to _____ _____ and start climbing the corporate ladder.

14. Mid-career movie stars often hit the reset button on their careers by doing _____ and taking jobs as product pitchmen.

15. After we pull out all the stops, the client is going to be _____ _____ and revenues will be through the roof.

## 11.C ➜ The Story Continues

**Task** ➜ Read the rest of the conversation, then answer the questions.

Judy:     Should we take out a bank loan to cover short-term costs?

Joan:     That won't be necessary. Our cash flow is fine. I just signed Hermes H2O.

Judy:     Really? How did you pull that off?

Joan:     Let's just say I have a knack for persuading people. I have a few more irons in the fire as well. One is with BMW.

Judy:     Wow. You are on a roll. Have you announced it?

Joan:     No. You can send out a memo about Hermes H2O, but Mum's the word on BMW. Like I said, let's not count our chickens before they're hatched.

Judy:     Does the BMW account come with any, you know, freebies?

Joan:     Like what? A few complimentary cars? I don't think so. What it does have is cachet. And that you can take to the bank.

## Questions

1. How many idioms can you identify in the passage above? What does each mean? Compare your choices to those on pg. 171. For definitions, see the word list, pg. 188.

2. Why is Joan on a roll? Explain.

3. Joan says BMW has cachet. What is cachet? Why do some products have it and others do not? Explain.

4. Joan says, "You don't get a second chance to make a first impression." Do you agree or disagree? When might this axiom not apply? What is your favorite axiom? Explain.

5. Verbally summarize this lesson. Time yourself. You have 2 minutes.

## 11.D ➔ Expansion

**Task** ➔ Match the expressions in column A with the definitions in column B.

| A | B |
|---|---|

1) have one's ducks in a row (to) ____

2) economic bubble (an) ____

3) in one's sights (to be) ____

4) fly in the face of something (to) ____

5) fly on the wall (to be a) ____

6) do something on the fly (to) ____

7) fly-by-night ____

8) pull an all-nighter (to) ____

9) have an eye for something (to) ____

10) iron out something (to) ____

11) strike while the iron is hot (to) ____

12) rule with an iron fist (to) ____

13) iron fist in a velvet glove (an) ____

14) as tough as nails (to be) ____

15) run through something (to) ____

16) zero hour (to be) ____

17) ground zero (to be) ____

18) zero sum gain (a) ____

19) quid pro quo ____ (Latin)

20) strange bedfellows (to be) (S) ____


A) to run contrary to

B) to work all night

C) to control with absolute authority

D) to be diplomatic yet strict

E) the time something important begins

F) to be the center of action

G) a winner and a loser with no net change in total wealth/advantages

H) an unusual/unexpected association

I) to review/explain

J) to do without preparation; to wing it

K) to have a talent for

L) something for something

M) unjustified speculation that increases prices to unreasonable levels

N) to be aiming at a target/goal

O) to be here today, gone tomorrow

P) to be strong/determined

Q) to be a secret observer

R) to do immediately to gain the advantage

S) to correct/fix/resolve

T) to be organized

## 11.E ➔ Writing Practice

**Task** ➔ Write a sentence using each idiom.

1) make-over (a)

_____

2) stodgy (to be)

_____

3) fly (to)

_____

4) when push comes to shove

_____

5) nail something (to)

_____

6) sound like a broken record (to)

_____

7) have an eye for something (to)

_____

8) eat out of one's hand (to)

_____

9) count one's chickens before they are hatched (to not)

_____

10) have one's ducks in a row (to)

_____

11)   burst one's bubble (to)

_____

12)   set one's sights a little lower/higher (to)

_____

13)   strange bedfellows (to be) (S)

_____

14)   go over something with a fine-tooth comb (to)

_____

15)   at the eleventh hour

_____

## 11.F ➔ More Writing Practice

**Task** ➔ Write a short passage using as many idioms as you can from this lesson. The topic is your choice. Make it business-related if possible.

_____

_____

_____

_____

_____

_____

_____

_____

# <u>Lesson #12</u> ➜ *A Conflict of Interest*

➜ **2:30 p.m.** Judy meets up with Beth in the coffee room.

✱✱✱

<u>Judy</u>:    Beth can you <u>give me your two cents</u> on something?

<u>Beth</u>:    <u>Absolutely</u>. Let's walk and talk. So, what's up?

<u>Judy</u>:    I'm <u>giving the keynote</u> tonight at the Business Forum. They've asked me to speak about the challenges of rebuilding a company's image after a scandal. They've asked me to speak about Testa Pharmaceuticals. As you know, Testa had a little problem with quality control a few months back.

<u>Beth</u>:    That little problem killed five people. So?

<u>Judy</u>:    As you know, my husband William works for Testa. He's the <u>general counsel</u>.

<u>Beth</u>:    Are you worried about <u>a conflict of interest</u>?

<u>Judy</u>:    Yes. Because Testa is our client, I have <u>to spin them in a positive light</u> even though everyone knows the company is still <u>treading water</u>.

<u>Beth</u>:    Was William involved in the scandal?

<u>Judy</u>:    No. His hands <u>are clean</u>. The issue was a foreign-based source. It sold <u>tainted</u> material to Testa. Why Testa's quality control missed it, I don't know. It's not exactly <u>a feather in their cap</u>.

<u>Beth</u>:    I see what you're <u>driving at</u>. The market knows that Testa <u>dropped the ball</u> and is still trying <u>to make amends</u>. Yet if you spin Testa in a positive light, some might think you're <u>pulling the wool over their eyes</u> because your husband works there and Testa is our client.

<u>Judy</u>:    Exactly. So is that a conflict of interest?

<u>Beth</u>:    Sounds like <u>a Catch-22</u> to me.

<u>Judy</u>:    So what should I do?

<u>Beth</u>:    I think you need a second opinion. Ask your William. After all, he is a lawyer.

<u>Judy</u>:    Right. The only problem is...

<u>Beth</u>:    Is what? Judy?

## 12.A ➜ Definitions

1) *give someone one's two cents (to)*
   - to express one's opinion

2) *absolutely*
   - yes/of course/certainly/by all means

3) *give the keynote (address) (to)*
   - to give the main speech/talk, etc.

4) *general counsel (the)*
   - the lawyer who heads the legal dept.

5) *conflict of interest (a)*
   - representing two opposing parties with different/conflicting interests

6) *spin someone/something in a positive light (to)*
   - to describe favorably in a way that runs contrary to the evidence

7) *tread water (to)*
   - to swim in one place; to lack progress; to spin one's wheels

8) *clean (to be)*
   - to be free of corruption/blame

9) *tainted (to be)*
   - to be infected/contaminated/corrupted

10) *have a feather in one's cap (to)*
    - to have a distinctive achievement

11) *driving at (to be)*
    - to be making a point/aiming at

12) *drop the ball (to)*
    - to fail to perform as expected

13) *make amends (to)*
    - to compensate for negligent behavior

14) *pull the wool over one's eyes (to)*
    - to fool/cheat someone

15) *Catch-22 (a)*
    - to be faced with two bad choices; a no-win situation

## 12.B ➜ Practice

**Task** ➜ Fill in the blanks using the idioms on the previous page.

1. When push comes to shove, we will seal the deal. _____ .

2. We've pulled out all the stops, but we are still _____ .

3. Jill climbed the corporate ladder until she finally became the _____ .

4. Al asked if I would _____ on his latest invention. I did and told him it was half-baked and would never fly.

5. Sue just got the green light to go to Viet Nam to open a new branch office. That's a real _____ , especially in this old boys' club.

6. You just bought a new house and you need to buy a new car? What exactly are you _____ ? I take it you want a raise.

7. That guy is a bad penny. His hands _____ definitely not _____ .

8. Helena is in _____ . If she works, she won't be able to finish school, but if she doesn't work, she won't be able to pay for school.

9. Dirk went over the contract with a fine-tooth comb, but I've already found three points that aren't boilerplate. Boy, did he _____ .

10. The smell from that factory has really _____ the air.

11. Mary just got a pink slip. She's not worried. She's _____ _____ . She thinks a change of companies will do her good.

12. It was high time Toni _____ for losing the account.

13. I would love to work for Apple and Microsoft at the same time. Who wouldn't? But that, I'm afraid, would be _____ .

14. Who is _____ at the conference? Rumor has it that Bill Gates is slated to speak. I would love to schmooze with him after.

15. Stop trying _____ . I wasn't born yesterday.

## 12.C → The Story Continues

**Task** → Read the rest of the conversation, then answer the questions.

Judy:   William and I had a falling out.

Beth:   Over what?

Judy:   Over where Debbie should go to university next year. William wants her to go to Princeton. She got accepted, but the tuition is outrageous.

Beth:   Okay, so apply for a student loan.

Judy:   Right. And when Debbie—who has never had a real job in a her life—graduates at 22, she'll be in debt to the tune of two-hundred thousand dollars. That is so criminal. The education system in this country makes me so mad. Kids are graduating with massive loans. How are they supposed to buy cars and houses, and start families when they're already saddled with so much debt? Once a university degree meant something, but now? In this economy? Ridiculous. And Washington is doing nothing about it. All they care about is getting re-elected by serving their corporate masters.

Beth:   Those corporate masters pay our salaries. But I do see what you're driving at. These days universities are simply brands, like a pair of jeans or sneakers. That said, at the end of the day, does Debbie want Princeton on her résumé or some no-name college?

Judy:   That's exactly what William said.

## Questions

1. How many idioms can you identify in the passage above? What does each mean? Compare your choices to those on pg. 172. For definitions, see the word list, pg.188.

2. Why did Judy and William have a falling out? Explain.

3. Is it better to get legal advice from a family member or from a third party? What about medical and financial advice? Explain.

4. Why is a college education in the U.S. so expensive? What about in your country? Explain.

5. Verbally summarize this lesson. Time yourself. You have 2 minutes.

## 12.D → Expansion

**Task** → Match the expressions in column A with the definitions in column B.

**A**

**B**

1) You bet. ____

2) kerfuffle (a) ____

3) euphemism (a) ____

4) preach to the choir (to) ____

5) pick one's brain (to) ____

6) spin doctor (a) ____

7) spin off (a) ____

8) in my heart of hearts... (S) ____

9) have a notch on one's belt (to) ____

10) caveat emptor ____ (Latin)

11) ad nauseum ____ (Latin)

12) modus operandi ____ (Latin)

13) status quo (the) ____ (Latin)

14) moratorium ____ (Latin)

15) ad hoc ____ (Latin)

16) wolf in sheep's clothing (a) ____

17) amendment (an) ____

18) have the upper hand (to) ____

19) go hand-in-hand (to) ____

20) hand it to someone (to) ____

A) Sure. Absolutely. Definitely

B) a product(s) developed from a successful product

C) to know deep within your heart/soul

D) to repeat endlessly

E) method of operation; M.O.

F) the current situation/state of affairs

G) an official waiting period in which amendments are sought or made

H) temporarily for a specific purpose

I) an adjustment/correction

J) to have the advantage

K) a disagreement/commotion/fuss

L) to give someone credit/kudos

M) Let the buyer beware.

N) a diplomatic word/comment replacing one that might offend/reflect negatively

O) to try and persuade an audience that already supports/agrees with you

P) to ask one a series of questions for clarification/feedback

Q) one who favorably promotes the actions/opinions of an individual/organization

R) to have a feather in one's cap

S) to go together; a logical connection

T) one who appears harmless but is in fact ruthless/dangerous

## 12.E ➔ Writing Practice

**Task** ➔ Write a sentence using each idiom.

1)  give someone one's two cents (to)

_____

2)  absolutely

_____

3)  go hand-in-hand (to)

_____

4)  in my heart of hearts (S)

_____

5)  conflict of interest (a)

_____

6)  spin someone/something in a positive light (to)

_____

7)  tread water (to)

_____

8)  caveat emptor

_____

9)  modus operandi

_____

10)  have a feather in one's cap (to)

_____

11)  driving at (to be)

_____

12)  drop the ball (to)

_____

13)  pick one's brain (to)

_____

14)  pull the wool over one's eyes (to)

_____

15)  Catch-22 (a)

_____

## 12.F → More Writing Practice

**Task** → Write a short passage using as many idioms as you can from this lesson. The topic is your choice. Make it business-related if possible.

_____

_____

_____

_____

_____

_____

_____

_____

_____

# Review #3

**Task** ➜ Fill in the blanks using the following idioms.

1. drop the ball
2. general counsel
3. You know the drill.
4. fly
5. a spin doctor
6. eat out of one's hand
7. burst one's bubble
8. at the eleventh hour
9. give the keynote
10. half-baked
11. green light
12. the suits
13. nail
14. pan
15. under the gun
16. old boys' club
17. a make-over
18. driving at
19. sound like a broken record
20. stodgy
21. overhaul
22. conflict of interest
23. tread water
24. set one's sights a little higher
25. pull the wool over one's eyes
26. pinching pennies
27. make amends

1. I hate to _____ , but you need to
   _____ for _____ last week.

2. You really need to talk to the _____ . That is definitely a
   _____ . She will give you the bottom line.

3. I know what you are _____ . Sorry, but I still think it
   is a _____ idea. It flies in the face of what _____ want.

4. I'm _____ speech at the conference.
   It is really going to _____ . I have definitely _____ it.

5. That guy is _____ . He's so glib. It's like he's
   always trying to _____ our _____ .

6. I hate to _____ but that suit is really _____ . What
   you need is _____ .

7. If you don't _____ , you will just _____ .

8. Don't do a thing until you get the _____ . _____ .
   And watch your budget. The company is really _____ .

9. Alice _____ my idea _____ . I really thought
   that I had her _____ . I guess not.

10. The government is _____ to _____ the _____
    _____ that is Wall Street.

# <u>Lesson #13</u> ➜ *Taking the Reins*

➜ **3:00 p.m.** Maria enters Joan's office.

✱✱✱

Maria:   Here is the <u>copy</u> for the new Heineken spot.

Joan:    Thanks. Just put it over there.

Maria:   Have you thought about what we talked about?

Joan:    What did we talk about? <u>Jog my memory</u>.

Maria:   A raise. You said you'd <u>mull it over</u> and get back to me.

Joan:    It <u>slipped my mind</u>. Sorry, I've been absolutely <u>swamped</u> lately.

Maria:   So?

Joan:    We're <u>strapped for cash</u>, you know that.

Maria:   I also know we're signing new clients <u>hand over fist</u>. Joan, you know I love working here. I have the best job in the world and the best boss too. You're so kind and considerate. And I've learned so much from you. You're a great teacher. The best. Better than all my MBA professors combined. Honest. It would kill me to work for somebody else. Nobody else has your <u>can-do attitude</u>. Nobody.

Joan:    Okay. Okay. You've <u>stroked my ego</u> enough. So, <u>here's the deal</u>. I think you <u>have got what it takes</u> to work with clients face-to-face. That said, how would you like to be an account executive? You will be responsible for our Latin American <u>division</u>.

Maria:   We have a Latin American division?

Joan:    We do now.

Maria:   Oh, my God. You want me <u>to take the reins</u>? Really?

Joan:    Absolutely. It's high time you stepped up to the plate. You have a knack for persuading. I've seen you in action. You can <u>charm the birds out of the trees</u>. What's wrong? <u>Cold feet</u>?

## 13.A → Definitions

1) *copy*
   - script; the written part of an ad

2) *jog one's memory (to)*
   - to help one remember

3) *mull something over (to)*
   - to think about; to consider carefully

4) *slip one's mind (to)*
   - to forget

5) *swamped (with something) (to be)*
   - to be overwhelmed with work

6) *strapped for something (to be)*
   - to be low on something; to have no extra money/time, etc.

7) *hand over fist*
   - done quickly in succession

8) *can-do attitude (a)*
   - the belief that nothing is impossible

9) *stroke one's ego (to)*
   - to flatter; to butter up

10) *here's the deal...*
    - this is the bottom line...

11) *have (got) what it takes (to)*
    - to have the ability/talent to succeed

12) *division*
    - department; section

13) *take the reins (to)*
    - to take control; to manage

14) *charm the birds out of the trees (to)*
    - to persuade anyone of anything

15) *have (get) cold feet (to)*
    - to be nervous/reluctant/doubting

## 13.B ➜ Practice

**Task ➜** Fill in the blanks using the idioms on the previous page.

1. Please _____ . I can't remember who was on that ad hoc committee.

2. Bill has _____ . That's his M.O. As a result, he is always pulling out all the stops to climb the corporate ladder.

3. _____ . At this company, you can't argue with the status quo. The boss is the boss, and she's as tough as nails.

4. Barry was so _____ with work, he had to pull an all-nighter.

5. The company pulled the plug on its investment banking _____ due to severe losses in the 2008 mortgage melt down.

6. Jack is such a yes-man. He _____ the CEO's _____ ad nauseum.

7. Sorry, but you're barking up the wrong tree. I'd love to lend you a million dollars, but I'm really _____ cash.

8. Before you buy that "pre-owned" BMW on eBay, you'd better take some time and _____ . Remember what they say: caveat emptor.

9. We've got to hand it to Beth. When the new accountant suddenly jumped ship, Beth stepped up to the plate and _____ .

10. I'd love to hob knob with Brad Clooney and his new wife, but I know I'd get _____ . I'm not much of a schmoozer. It's just not my M.O.

11. We struck while the iron was hot and now we're raking money in _____ _____ . At this rate, we will be in the black by next quarter.

12. Hank burned the midnight oil writing _____ for the new KFC TV spot.

13. You can pick my brain all you want, but I'm telling you, it has completely _____ .

14. Joe is so smooth. He can _____ .

15. _____ you _____ to swim with sharks?

## 13.C → The Story Continues

**Task** → Read the rest of the conversation, then answer the questions.

Maria:  Cold feet? No. Not at all. I'm definitely up for this. Totally.

Joan:  Good. When you walk out of this office, I want you to hit the ground running. Here's a list of major corporations in Latin America.

Maria:  Wow. So many.

Joan:  That's just for starters. Call them up. Give them the elevator pitch. Tell them that Austen Advertising is poised to take them to the next level with the best creative team in the business and a financial staff second to none. Don't hang up until you get your foot in the door. Offer them lunch, dinner. Whatever it takes. You have to convince them that we are the only game in town.

Maria:  This is so unexpected. Really. I don't know how to thank you.

Joan:  Don't. You deserve it. You've always gone the extra mile. When it's crunch time, you've always come through. Anything else?

Maria:  Yes. Does this mean I get a raise?

Joan:  Bring me some good news and we'll talk. Oh, and you'll need to find and train a replacement—and get yourself an assistant.

## Questions

1. How many idioms can you identify in the passage above? What does each mean? Compare your choices to those on pg. 174. For definitions, see the word list, pg. 188.

2. Did Maria get what she wanted? Explain.

3. If you were promoted, and your new job were overseas, would you accept the position? On what conditions would you not work abroad? Explain.

4. Considering Maria's background and work experience, do you think Joan is taking a risk promoting her to such a high position? Explain.

5. Verbally summarize this lesson. Time yourself. You have 2 minutes.

## 13.D ➔ Expansion

**Task** ➔ Match the expressions in column A with the definitions in column B.

**A**

**B**

1) ruminate (to) ____

2) slipshod (to be) ____

3) cut corners (to) ____

4) deal breaker (a) ____

5) rein in something (to) ____

6) rainmaker (a) ____

7) snowed under (to be) ____

8) good for one's ego (to be) ____

9) on an ego-trip (to be) ____

10) win hands-down (to) ____

11) lend a hand (to) ____

12) hold all the cards (to) ____

13) turn the tables (to) ____

14) tight-fisted (to be) ____

15) have a burr under one's saddle (to) ____

16) have butterflies in one's stomach (to) ____

17) take the high road (to) ____

18) too much of a good thing ____ (S)

19) down to the wire (to be) ____

20) have wiggle room (to) ____

A) to be of poor quality

B) to reduce/limit by strict control

C) to be good for one's self-esteem

D) negative consequences arising from enjoying something for too long

E) to be in the best position to win/gain

F) to have room to negotiate; to be flexible

G) to do what is best/honest/ethical

H) to mull it over

I) to reverse positions and gain the advantage

J) to be nervous

K) to offer help

L) to be miserly/frugal/cheap

M) to make a fuss

N) to be crunch time/zero hour

O) an issue that stops one or both parties from sealing a deal

P) to be blowing one's horn ad nauseum

Q) to be swamped

R) a money-maker

S) to reduce costs by using inferior material/bypassing accepted practices

T) to win decisively

## 13.E ➔ Writing Practice

**Task** ➔ Write a sentence using each idiom.

1) have butterflies in one's stomach (to)

_____

2) jog one's memory (to)

_____

3) mull something over (to)

_____

4) slip one's mind (to)

_____

5) swamped (to be)

_____

6) strapped for something (to be)

_____

7) good for one's ego (to be)

_____

8) can-do attitude (a)

_____

9) lend a hand (to)

_____

10) down to the wire (to be)

_____

11) have got what it takes (to)

_____

12) tight-fisted (to be)

_____

13) take the reins (to)

_____

14) snowed under (to be)

_____

15) cut corners (to)

_____

## 13.F ➜ More Writing Practice

**Task** ➜ Write a short passage using as many idioms as you can from this lesson. The topic is your choice. Make it business-related if possible.

_____

_____

_____

_____

_____

_____

_____

_____

# Lesson #14 ➔ *The New Normal*

➔ **3:30 p.m.** Joan works at her desk. The phone rings. It's Maria.

✳✳✳

Joan:     Yes, Maria?

Maria:    Abby Finestein is on the line.

Joan:     Thanks. Put her through. Hi, Abby? What's up?

Abby:     *(on the phone )* Joanie, darling, drop everything. I've found what you're looking for. It just came on the market. It's on Central Park West and it is <u>to die for</u>. Can you <u>squeeze in a look</u>?

Joan:     Central Park West? That's a little out of my league.

Abby:     Just <u>keep an open mind</u>. Believe me, it will be <u>love at first sight</u>.

Joan:     I'm sorry, I'm swamped. Really. Can we <u>hook up</u> tomorrow?

Abby:     Tomorrow will be too late. Believe me, you pass on this gem and you'll be <u>kicking yourself for the rest of your life</u>.

Joan:     When was it <u>listed</u>?

Abby:     This morning.

Joan:     I'll be right over. What's the address?

          *(Later Abby shows Joan the apartment.)*

Abby:     See? Didn't I tell you? This place has the both of best worlds: old world charm with a high-tech interior. Everything is <u>state-of-the-art</u>. These people really went to town. Don't you love all the <u>bells and whistles</u>?

Joan:     A TV in the shower?

Abby:     It's <u>the new normal</u>. Everybody's got one. Look at that view. It's got success <u>written all over it</u>.

Joan:     The price is <u>a bit steep</u>. Is there any wiggle room?

Abby:     Sorry. Like I said, it's <u>a seller's market</u>. And believe me, the market is red-hot. If you don't <u>grab it</u>, the next guy will. Wall Street just got their bonuses. <u>When word gets out</u>, this place will be gone in a New-York minute.

## 14.A → Definitions

1) *die for (to)*
   - to desire at any cost
   _____

2) *squeeze in a look (at) (to)*
   - to make time to see something
   _____

3) *keep an open mind (to)*
   - to be understanding; to not prejudge
   _____

4) *love at first sight (to be)*
   - to feel an instant attraction for
   _____

5) *hook up (with) (to)*
   - to meet (with)
   _____

6) *kick oneself for the rest of one's life (to)*
   - to regret always
   _____

7) *list (to)*
   - to put a property on the market
   _____

8) *state-of-the-art (to be)*
   - to be the best design/technology, etc.
   available at the time
   _____

9) *bells and whistles*
   - extra features
   _____

10) *the new normal*
    - the new standard/practice
    _____

11) *written all over someone/thing (to be)*
    - to be reflected in; to symbolize
    _____

12) *bit (too) steep (to be a)*
    - to be (too) expensive
    _____

13) *seller's market (a)*
    - a market in which sellers can set the
    price due to limited inventory
    _____

14) *grab something (to)*
    - to buy quickly
    _____

15) *when word gets out (that)...*
    - when many learn of the fact...
    _____

## 14.B → Practice

**Task** → Fill in the blanks using the idioms on the previous page.

1. Working from home is quickly becoming _____ .

2. Patti and Lily are going _____ over a working lunch to iron out the details in the letter-of-intent.

3. A bull market is _____ . Caveat emptor.

4. Joe, I know you always take no prisoners, but when you meet with the IRS next week, please _____ .

5. I ran the numbers and, unfortunately, the PSF is _____ . Is there any wiggle room?

6. Ann looks like the cat that ate the canary. It's _____
_____ .

7. If you like that apartment, you'd better _____ . Seriously. In this neck of the woods, it will be gone in a New York minute.

8. Living in Manhattan is _____ . Absolutely. If that is your dream, then you'd better start climbing the corporate ladder.

9. During lunch, Elvia was able _____ the new Audi over at the dealer's. She thinks it's a steal. I beg to differ.

10. When Swati saw the new iPad, it was _____ .

11. _____ we won't be getting bonuses this year, more than a few are going to hit the roof.

12. Car dealers always peddle the car with the most _____ .

13. Stop being so wishy-washy. If you don't step up to the plate and bid on that contract, you are going _____ .

14. On TV, _____ products, like the new Cadillac, are pitched using soft selling.

15. The best time _____ a house is in early spring.

## 14.C ➜ The Story Continues

**Task** ➜ Read the rest of the conversation, then answer the questions.

Joan:    This place is much bigger than I need. Is the one in Tribeca still available?

Abby:    Forget Tribeca. Trust me, in the long run, this place will give you more bang for your buck. Central Park West always sells even when the market tanks. It's money in the bank, believe me. And remember: a bird in hand is worth two in the bush.

Joan:    It is rather nice. It should be for what they're asking.

Abby:    Joanie, I hate to beat a dead horse, but it's high noon*, honey.

Joan:    What about parking?

Abby:    You get a space in the basement. Totally secure. (*Her cell phone rings, and rings*). The clock's running, Joanie. The wolves are at the door.

Joan:    I'll take it.

Abby:    Good girl. You won't regret it. This place is you all over.

Joan:    Will they knock five percent off if I pay cash?

Abby:    No harm in asking. What about your Greenwich place?

Joan:    List it. It's time to move on.

## Questions

1. How many idioms can you identify in the passage above? What does each mean? Compare your choices to those on pg. 176. For definitions, see the word list, pg. 188.

2. What does Joan decide to list? Why? Explain.

3. Have you ever experienced love at first sight? Explain.

4. Abby says a TV in the shower is the new normal. What is the new normal in your country and in the U.S.? Explain.

5. Verbally summarize this lesson. Time yourself. You have 2 minutes.

*\* See Movie-TV quotes pg. 214*

## 14.D → Expansion

**Task** → Match the expressions in column A with the definitions in column B.

**A**

**B**

1)  co-op (a) ____

2)  walk-up (a) ____

3)  penthouse (a) ____

4)  condo (a) ____

5)  trust fund (a) ____

6)  upmarket (to be) ____

7)  nouveau riche (to be) ____

8)  old money (to be) ____

9)  have curb appeal (to) ____

10) fixer-upper (a) ____

11) brick-and-mortar (a) ____

12) lien (a) ____

13) Location, location, location. ____

14) white elephant (a) ____

15) forfeiture ____

16) trust-fund baby (a) ____

17) buyer's market (a) ____

18) flip (to) ____

19) escrow account (an) ____

20) All that glitters is not gold.
____ (S)

A)  real estate rule #1

B)  property that sits empty because it will not sell due to price/location, etc.

C)  apartment or house with no elevator

D)  a market with high inventory resulting in competitive prices

E)  rich within one's own generation

F)  building in which individual units are privately owned

G)  luxury apartment on the top floor

H)  the loss of property as a result of default

I)  to be historically wealthy

J)  legal holding containing assets benefiting an individual/organization

K)  residential building owned and managed by the residents

L)  rich from inheriting a trust fund

M)  to buy then immediately sell for a profit

N)  account in which the monies of two parties is monitored by a third party

O)  to look desirable from the street

P)  a legal claim on a property

Q)  a traditional store

R)  a listed residence needing work

S)  to be luxurious/expensive/upscale

T)  Don't judge a book by its cover.

## 14.E → Writing Practice

**Task** → Write a sentence using each idiom.

1) die for (to)

_____

2) squeeze in a look (at) (to)

_____

3) keep an open mind (to)

_____

4) love at first sight (to be)

_____

5) hook up (with) (to)

_____

6) kick oneself for the rest of one's life (to)

_____

7) state-of-the-art (to be)

_____

8) brick-and-mortar (a)

_____

9) bells and whistles

_____

10) the new normal

_____

11) written all over someone/thing (to be)

_____

12) bit (too) steep (to be a)

_____

13) a seller's market

_____

14) grab something (to)

_____

15) buyer's market (a)

_____

## 14.F ➔ More Writing Practice

**Task** ➔ Write a short passage using as many idioms as you can from this lesson. The topic is your choice. Make it business-related if possible.

_____

_____

_____

_____

_____

_____

_____

_____

_____

# Lesson #15 ➜ *No Free Lunch*

➜ **3:50 p.m.** Rick and Beth discuss Rick's script for a Hammett Hotels spot.

✷✷✷

Rick: So what do you think? Is it <u>ready for prime time</u>?

Beth: I think you need to use a spell checker. Hammett has two T's and two M's.

Rick: Really?

Beth: Really. Hammett. H for hotel. A for alpha. M for Mike. M for Mike. E for echo. T for tango. T for tango. Next time remember <u>to dot your i's and cross your t's</u>. Mrs. Hammett is <u>a stickler for detail</u>.

Rick: Tell me about it. That woman is <u>the bane of my existence</u>. She rejected everything I wrote for her last campaign.

Beth: Mrs. H. is <u>nothing if not predictable</u>.

Rick: Okay, so what's the bottom line on this spot?

Beth: First off, Hammett is not <u>catering to</u> your average <u>road warrior</u>. Hammett is an upscale <u>niche market</u>. People who stay at Hammett are not pinching pennies. They are <u>movers and shakers</u> with Gulfstreams. Everything about them screams success. That said, I'm taking you off this account. I'm sorry it didn't pan out.

Rick: So you're throwing me under the bus?

Beth: I'm sorry, but <u>my hands are tied</u>. Mrs. Hammett <u>calls the shots</u> and she wants a new copywriter. Remember, this is not personal. It's business.

Rick: I understand. Actually, I'm glad to be off this account. I know Mrs. H. runs a tight ship, but you can't expect a miracle on <u>a shoe-string budget</u>. If she wants sophistication and eloquence, she's going to have <u>to pony up</u>. If not, the competition will eat her lunch.

Beth: Believe me, I've told her that a million times. It goes in one ear and out the other. Old money is like that. They march to the beat of their own drummer.

Rick: Yeah, well, rich or not, tell her there's <u>no free lunch</u>. Speaking of lunch, are you hungry?

Beth: Starving. Let's grab a bite. By the way, you did <u>a bang-up job on the Dairy Queen spot</u>. You really hit it out of the park.

## 15.A → Definitions

1) *ready for prime time (to be)*
   - to be ready to step up to the plate; to be ready to be presented/sold, etc.

2) *dot one's i's and cross one's t's (to)*
   - to check for detail errors; to go over with a fine-tooth comb

3) *stickler for detail (to be a)*
   - one who demands perfection

4) *bane of one's existence (the)*
   - something that causes one constant problems/pressure/headaches

5) *nothing if not predictable (to be)*
   - to be predictable

6) *cater (to)*
   - to serve/provide what is needed

7) *road warrior (a)*
   - one who is always traveling for business

8) *niche market (a)*
   - a small specialized market

9) *movers and shakers*
   - those with power and influence

10) *my hands are tied*
    - I have no freedom to influence or control.

11) *call the shots (to)*
    - to give orders

12) *shoe-string budget (a)*
    - a budget set as low as possible

13) *pony up (to)*
    - to pay what is owed/needed

14) *no free lunch (there is)*
    - nothing is free

15) *bang-up job (a)*
    - a job well done

## 15.B → Practice

**Task** → Fill in the blanks using the idioms on the previous page.

1.  If I were you, I'd fix up your house, then list it. Right now, it's not _____ _____ .

2.  Tom might be able to charm the birds out of the trees, but in his monthly reports, he never _____ .

3.  Joan does not want back-of-the-envelope calculations. She is _____ _____ . Please give her the final numbers.

4.  Another upgrade? That's the second one this year. Microsoft is _____ _____ .

5.  The Waldorf Astoria _____ the noveau riche and to old money.

6.  _____ love freebies because they are usually on tight budgets.

7.  Retailers who target _____ are closed on Black Friday.

8.  I'm _____ around here. It's either my way or the highway.

9.  At the eleventh hour, the board _____ the cash needed to complete the project on time.

10. I'd love to give you a corner office, but _____ .

11. Once a year, the world's _____ meet in Davos, Switzerland to discus world problems and to schmooze.

12. This laptop is _____ . It is always crashing. I wish Dell would step up to the plate and replace it.

13. It's high time we gave Maria a raise. Since she came on board, she's been doing _____ . She has a real can-do attitude.

14. Sorry, but we can't make lemonade out of lemons on _____ .

15. In this firm, there are _____ . At the end of the day, bill the client for everything—pencils, stamps, coffee—the works.

## 15.C ➜ The Story Continues

**Task** ➜ Read the rest of the conversation, then answer the questions.

*(Later Rick and Beth eat pizza at a pizza joint.)*

Rick: When I grabbed a coffee at Mickey-D's this morning, I noticed that they've got oatmeal and blueberries on the menu.

Beth: Healthy fast-food is the new normal. Fast-food chains are waking up to the fact that their customers are becoming more health conscious. Did you know that eight million Americans have diabetes and that 79 million have prediabetes?

Rick: Amazing.

Beth: High-fructose corn syrup is the culprit. It's in everything. I don't touch the stuff. I read every label before I buy.

Rick: You on a diet?

Beth: Isn't everyone? So what was the coffee like?

Rick: At Mickey D's? Great. It wasn't run-of-the-mill at all. It was a medium roast. For a buck, you can get a small, medium or large. Your choice for a buck! I don't know how Starbucks competes. They're pricing themselves out of the market. What?

Beth: Are you going to eat that last slice?

Rick: Knock yourself out.

## Questions

1. How many idioms can you identify in the passage above? What does each mean? Compare your choices to those on pg. 177. For definitions, see the word list, pg. 188.

2. Why does Rick say to Beth *knock yourself out*? Explain.

3. Fast-food is a major health problem in the U.S. What about in your country? Why is it a problem? What is the solution? Explain.

4. Hammett Hotels is a niche market. What are some other niche markets, upscale and otherwise? Explain.

5. Verbally summarize this lesson. Time yourself. You have <u>2</u> minutes.

## 15.D → Expansion

**Task** → Match the expressions in column A with the definitions in column B.

**A**

**B**

1)  anal (to be) ___

2)  corner the market (to) ___

3)  flood the market (to) ___

4)  flea market (a) ___

5)  fringe benefits ___

6)  dismiss (to) ___

7)  can (to) ___

8)  pull oneself up by one's bootstraps (to) ___

9)  put oneself in another's shoes (to) ___

10) If the shoe fits, wear it. ___

11) shoe is on the other foot (the) ___

12) wait for the other shoe to drop (to) ___

13) shoe-in (a) ___

14) tower of strength (to be a) ___ (S)

15) shot (a) ___

16) long shot (a) ___

17) end with a bang (to) ___

18) open with a bang (to) ___

19) bang-on (to be) ___

20) bang the drum (to) ___

A)  incentives not included in a salary; bonus/perks

B)  to let go/release from duties

C)  If it works, do it/go for it.

D)  to wait for more bad news

E)  a definite winner

F)  to be a symbol of power/resolve

G)  to control all parts of a market

H)  to oversupply a market with the same product

I)  a chance

J)  having little or no chance of success

K)  to start with power/excitement

L)  to be perfect/exact

M)  an antique/used-goods market

N)  to consider from a new/different perspective

O)  to fire/axe

P)  to finish with power/excitement

Q)  to be a stickler for detail

R)  to improve one's situation by one's own efforts

S)  to support/promote enthusiastically

T)  the tables have been turned

## 15.E → Writing Practice

**Task** → Write a sentence using each idiom.

1) ready for prime time (to be)

_____

2) dot your i's and cross your t's (to)

_____

3) stickler for detail (to be a)

_____

4) bane of one's existence (the)

_____

5) nothing if not predictable (to be)

_____

6) cater (to)

_____

7) road warrior (a)

_____

8) niche market (a)

_____

9) long shot (a)

_____

10) have one's hands tied (to)

_____

11) call the shots (to)

_____

12) shoe-string budget (a)

_____

13) pony up (to)

_____

14) no free lunch (there is)

_____

15) bang-up job (a)

_____

## 15.F ➔ More Writing Practice

**Task** ➔ Write a short passage using as many idioms as you can from this lesson. The topic is your choice. Make it business-related if possible.

_____

_____

_____

_____

_____

_____

_____

_____

# <u>Lesson #16</u> ➔ *Pushing my Buttons*

➔ **4:30 p.m.** Joan is typing at her desk when her computer suddenly freezes.

★ ★ ★

Joan:     I can't believe it. This thing is really <u>pushing my buttons</u>. Arg! Maria?

Maria:    (*entering*) Did your computer crash again?

Joan:     Yes. Get Hector before I <u>have a melt down</u>.

Maria:    Did you try rebooting?

Joan:     Rebooting is <u>for the birds</u>.

Hector:   (*entering*) I heard screaming.

Joan:     My computer crashed again. That's the third time this week.

Hector:   Did you try rebooting?

Joan:     Yes. This is <u>the last straw</u>. I'm sick and tired of Microsoft always updating. They say you can do things with fewer clicks. Instead, they just screw things up. I'm sorry but I don't have time to learn their latest upgrades. Why can't Bill Gates <u>leave well enough alone</u>? Doesn't he realize that he's <u>shooting himself in the foot</u>?

Maria:    <u>If it ain't broke, don't fix it</u>. That's what I always say.

Hector:   Can you <u>trace</u> the problem?

Joan:     The problem is Outlook Express. Every time I open it, it crashes. It used to be so easy and reliable. Now it <u>has a mind of its own</u>.

Maria:    The worse thing is Outlook's navigation. I'm always losing files.

Joan:     What about changing to Apple? I know you used to get more bang for your buck with Microsoft but all that's changed, right?

Hector:   Right. Apple is pretty much eating Microsoft's lunch. If you ask me, Microsoft has been resting on their laurels for too long. They used to be on the cutting-edge. Now they're just <u>fast-followers</u> making <u>me-too products</u>. Even then, they <u>don't deliver</u>, like Zune their MP3 player. What a dog. Okay. There you go. <u>Back in business</u>.

Joan:     Great. What did you do?

Hector:   Just a little <u>TLC</u>. You want me <u>to touch base with</u> the Apple rep?

## 16.A → Definitions

1)  *push one's buttons (to)*
    - to cause one to become annoyed/angry

2)  *have a meltdown (to)*
    - to have a loss of emotional control

3)  *for the birds (to be)*
    -to be a waste of time

4)  *last straw (the)*
    - the moment when the line has been crossed

5)  *leave well enough alone (to)*
    - to not touch

6)  *shoot oneself in the foot (to)*
    - to do/say something that negatively effects oneself

7)  *If it ain't (isn't) broke(n), don't fix it.*
    - Why mess with success? Why change a winning plan?

8)  *trace (to)*
    - to find/locate

9)  *have a mind of its own (to)*
    - to refuse to take orders

10) *fast-follower (a)*
    - one that copies successful ideas and profits from them

11) *me-too product (a)*
    - a product copied after a bestseller

12) *deliver (to)*
    - to perform as promised/expected

13) *back in business (to be)*
    - to be fixed; to be ready once again

14) *TLC*
    - tender-loving care

15) *touch base with someone (to)*
    - to meet/contact someone

## 16.B → Practice

**Task** → Fill in the blanks using the idioms on the previous page.

1.  Hector is a wiz at _____ computer problems.

2.  In Manhattan, trying to beat the traffic is _____ .

3.  No raise? Again? That's _____ . Tomorrow,
    I intend to jump ship. This accounting firm is not the only game in town.

4.  Let me lay it on the line. This company will never be _____ .
    We'll always make state-of-the-art products for an upscale, niche market.

5.  No, I did not _____ that company. Why
    not? Because they're small potatoes. We have much bigger fish to fry.

6.  Joe had _____ when Joan told him that his idea
    was half-baked. No surprise there. Joe is nothing if not predictable.

7.  What's good for my ego? When I _____ .

8.  Your report is great. A real bang-up job. You don't have to change a thing.
    _____ until you get more feedback.

9.  People who are anal often end up _____
    because they can never leave well enough alone.

10. If you want to take a shot at swimming with the sharks, you'd better leave the
    _____ at home. Trust me, heavy hitters take no prisoners.

11. I'm glad Diana is well and _____ . She has always been
    a tower of strength.

12. Tailgaters really _____ .

13. Ever since Apple introduced the iPad, the market has been flooded with
    _____ , many of which are sold at big-box stores.

14. Some say, "Upgrade." I say, " _____ ."

15. This printer is so slow. I swear, the thing _____ .

## 16.C ➜ The Story Continues

**Task** ➜ Read the rest of the conversation, then answer the questions.

Joan: Yes. Call the Apple rep. But don't sign anything before you bring me the numbers. I don't want to be taken to the cleaners, all right?

Hector: Understand. *(exiting)* Let me know if you have any more hiccups.

Joan: You'll be the first to know, believe me.

Maria: Joan? Aren't you lunching tomorrow with Sylvia Smith, Microsoft's V.P. of marketing?

Joan: I am. So?

Maria: So why don't you tell her enough with the upgrades? Serious. Somebody should do a productivity study and figure out how many working-hours employees lose every year wasting time trying to relearn software updates or waiting for updates to install.

Joan: Then what?

Maria: Then all those companies that have lost time should send the bill to Microsoft and sue for compensation.

## Questions

1. How many idioms can you identify in the passage above? What does each mean? Compare your choices to those on pg. 179. For definitions, see the word list, pg. 188.

2. Do you think Joan will act on Maria's advice? Why? Why not? Explain.

3. What problems have you had updating your home or office computer? Explain.

4. Cloud computing is the new normal. What is cloud computing? What are the pros and cons of cloud computing, for business and for the consumer? Explain.

5. Verbally summarize this lesson. Time yourself. You have <u>2</u> minutes.

## 16.D → Expansion

**Task** → Match the expressions in column A with the definitions in column B.

**A**

**B**

| | | | |
|---|---|---|---|
| 1) | hit the panic button (to) ____ | A) | to keep silent |
| 2) | arrive on the button (to) ____ | B) | to be easy; to have no effect |
| 3) | right on the button (to be) ____ | C) | an easy target |
| 4) | buttoned-down (to be) ____ | D) | to lose the ability to do something |
| 5) | cute as a button (to be) ____ | E) | to be uncertain/in doubt |
| 6) | button up (to) ____ | F) | to remember/consider |
| 7) | hot-button issue (a) ___ | G) | to admit defeat/a mistake |
| 8) | have one's finger on the button (to) ____ | H) | to be inclined to... |
| | | I) | to show up exactly at the right time |
| 9) | chicken feed (to be) ____ | J) | misrepresenting an opponent's position with false claims; informal fallacy |
| 10) | water off a duck's back (to be) ____ | K) | having a clear M.O. when one is thinking outside the box |
| 11) | sitting duck (a) ____ | |
| 12) | night owl (a) ____ | L) | to be conservative/traditional |
| 13) | eat crow (to) ____ | M) | a controversial topic |
| 14) | lose one's touch (to) ____ | N) | to guess with no information |
| 15) | touch-and-go (to be) ____ | O) | to lose emotional control; to freak out |
| 16) | grasp at straws (to) ____ | P) | to be in a position to control events |
| 17) | strawman argument (a) ____ | Q) | one who prefers the night |
| 18) | bear in mind (to) ____ | R) | a very small amount of money; chump change |
| 19) | method to [one's] madness [a] ____ (S) | |
| 20) | of a mind to... (to be) ____ | S) | to be cute/adorable |
| | | T) | to be exact/correct/spot on |

## 16.E → Writing Practice

**Task** → Write a sentence using each idiom.

1)  push one's buttons (to)

_____

2)  buttoned-down (to be)

_____

3)  for the birds (to be)

_____

4)  last straw (the)

_____

5)  leave well enough alone (to)

_____

6)  shoot oneself in the foot (to)

_____

7)  hot-button issue (a)

_____

8)  hit the panic button (to)

_____

9)  have a mind of its own (to)

_____

10)  fast-follower (a)

_____

11)  me-too product (a)

_____

12)  deliver (to)

_____

13)  eat crow (to)

_____

14)  bear in mind (to)

_____

15)  lose one's touch (to)

_____

## 16.F ➜ More Writing Practice

**Task** ➜ Write a short passage using as many idioms as you can from this
lesson. The topic is your choice. Make it business-related if possible.

_____

_____

_____

_____

_____

_____

_____

_____

## Review #4

**Task** ➜ Fill in the blanks using the following idioms.

| | | |
|---|---|---|
| 1. lend a hand | 10. penthouse | 19. strapped for cash |
| 2. buttoned-down | 11. rainmaker | 20. can-do attitude |
| 3. buyer's market | 12. mull it over | 21. take the reins |
| 4. hands down | 13. shoe-string budget | 22. nouveau riche |
| 5. stickler for details | 14. calls the shots | 23. method to one's madness |
| 6. cut corners | 15. touch base with | 24. down to the wire |
| 7. rein in | 16. pony up | 25. no free lunch |
| 8. hold all the cards | 17. hand-over-fist | 26. state-of-the-art |
| 9. to die for | 18. cater to | 27. the bane of my existence |

1.  Even though the company is _____ , everyone still has
    a _____ and is ready to _____ where needed.

2.  Ann is very _____ . In this office, she _____
    _____ and is a _____ .

3.  If you're living on a _____ , here's the deal.
    Avoid retailers that _____ the _____ .

4.  That _____ is _____ . Everything is
    _____ . Best of all, it's a _____ .

5.  There is definitely a _____ Chuck's _____ .
    There must be. He's making money _____ .

6.  We're going to win _____ because we _____ .

7.  I can't believe it. Manuel is a _____ , but he asked me to _____
    _____ for lunch. Doesn't that guy know there are _____ ?

8.  I asked Wioleta to _____ and _____ costs. I also
    told her to not _____ even if production is _____ .

9.  I _____ the client and gave her the pitch. She
    said she'd _____ and get back to me ASAP.

10. Staying on a diet is _____ .

# Lesson #17 ➜ *Legal Advice*

➜ **4:45 p.m.**  Joan calls Don at his office.

✱ ✱ ✱

Joan:    Don? Hi. It's Joan. Did I get you at a bad time?

Don:    Not at all. What can I do for you? Let me guess. You're calling because you'll finally let me take you out for dinner and a Yankee's game. So, what time should I pick you up Saturday?

Joan:    Sorry. This is strictly business, I'm afraid. I'll have to take a rain check.

Don:    I'm keeping track of all those rain checks, you know. So what's up?

Joan:    I need to bend your ear about something.

Don:    Absolutely.

Joan:    My agency is really taking off. We're moving to a new space and we'll be doubling our staff. We're also setting up shop in London and Beijing.

Don:    Wow. You really are firing on all cylinders, aren't you?

Joan:    Nothing ventured, nothing gained.

Don:    Indeed. So where do I fit in?

Joan:    Right now Austen Advertising is a sole proprietorship. In light of our current expansion, I was wondering if Austen should become a limited partnership, a corporation, or remain a sole proprietorship. In a nutshell, what are the arguments for each?

Don:    Well, as a sole proprietor—as you are now—you're responsible for everything. Moreover, there is no distinction between your assets and the company's assets. The upside is fewer regulations and no double taxation. However, if you are sued, you will lose your shirt, figuratively speaking, of course.

Joan:    What about a limited partnership?

Don:    In that case, you'd be the general partner, the boss basically. You'd still call the shots. Under you, there'd be limited partners. To become a limited partner, each individual would invest a specified amount in the partnership. They, in turn, would be liable only for the amount they invested.

Joan:    And a corporation?

## 17.A → Definitions

1) *bend one's ear (to)*
   - to ask for advice

2) *take off (to)*
   - to go up; to do well/succeed

3) *set up shop (in) (to)*
   - to open a business (in)

4) *fire on all cylinders (to)*
   - to work like a well-oiled engine

5) *fit in (to)*
   - to belong

6) *sole proprietorship (a)*
   - a business in which one assumes all
   the risks and benefits

7) *in light of...*
   - considering the fact that...

8) *limited partnership (a)*
   - a business that combines the features
   of a corporation and a partnership for
   tax shelter purposes

9) *corporation (a)*
   - a business that is a legal entity separate
   from its owners

10) *in a nutshell*
    - in brief; in short

11) *the upside is...*
    - the advantage is...

12) *lose one's shirt (to)*
    - to experience a significant loss

13) *figuratively speaking (to be)*
    - to be speaking metaphorically

14) *in turn*
    - as a result; it follows

15) *liable (to be)*
    - to be legally responsible/obligated

## 17.B ➜ Practice

**Task** ➜ Fill in the blanks using the idioms on the previous page.

1.  That idea is a long shot. If it doesn't fly, I will _____ .

2.  _____ , if the shoe fits, wear it.

3.  When you finally decide _____ , remember: location, location, location.

4.  Carla is a great boss. I'm always _____ about something.

5.  Many law firms are _____ .

6.  Anthony has always been a rainmaker, but lately his ideas have failed _____ . He seems to be spinning his wheels.

7.  Revenues are up. So is productivity. Employee morale is also hitting new highs. The company is definitely _____ .

8.  How does taking a trip to Hawaii _____ to your business plan? Run that by me again. I want to make sure we're on the same page.

9.  _____ the fact that their last offer was a deal breaker, I'm of a mind to pull the plug and go bang the drum elsewhere.

10. The bottom line is we need to build environmentally friendly oil rigs. If we don't, we are going _____ for every drop of oil we spill.

11. Mike, you will go and talk to the client. The client will, _____ , report back to Sally as to their final decision.

12. Sure, you got axed, but _____ you are now free to start your own business, you know, the one you've always talked about.

13. I've told Barney he should really incorporate to protect his personal assets, but he says _____ is all he really needs.

14. Many point to the Dutch East India Company as being the world's first

    _____ .

15. _____ , I think we have been fast-followers far too long. It is time to think outside the box and hit one out of the park.

## 17.C ➜ The Story Continues

**Task** ➜ Read the rest of the conversation, then answer the questions.

Don: With a corporation, you'd have to go public. You'd sell shares and basically be beholden to your shareholders. You'd have to get a bank to underwrite your IPO, hold annual shareholder meetings, and perform myriad other corporation functions all in the public eye. However, as a sole proprietor, you'd remain private, as you would with a limited partnership.

Joan: So what do you recommend?

Don: I recommend dinner and a Yankee's game. Between innings, I can elaborate on the finer points of each business entity. Shall I pencil you in for Saturday night?

Joan: You drive a hard bargain, counselor.

Don: I hate to rush you, but I have the Canadian ambassador parked on the other line.

Joan: What's he want?

Don: Sorry, attorney-client privilege. So, what's it going to be?

Joan: Well, since you did give me free legal advice, I will attend your soirée tonight. It's at the Waldorf, right?

Don: Yes. The party starts at 8:00. Do you need a lift?

Joan: I'm fine, thanks. I'll see you there.

## Questions

1. How many idioms can you identify in the passage above? What does each mean? Compare your choices to those on pg. 181. For definitions, see the word list, pg. 188.

2. In the end, what does Don recommend? Why? Explain.

3. If you were Joan, what business type would you chose? Why? Explain.

4. Explain the concept of attorney-client privilege. Why is such a privilege necessary for lawyers and clients, and for doctors and patients? Explain.

5. Verbally summarize this lesson. Time yourself. You have <u>2</u> minutes.

## 17.D → Expansion

**Task** → Match the expressions in column A with the definitions in column B.

**A**

1)  set off (to) ____

2)  all set (to be) ____

3)  fit the bill (to) ____

4)  play with fire (to) ____

5)  jump out of the frying pan and into the fire (to) ____

6)  get on like a house on fire (to) ____

7)  burning question (the) ____

8)  old flame (an) ____

9)  shoot down in flames (to) ____

10) burned (to be) ____

11) hard nut to crack (a) ____

12) nuts and bolts (the) ____

13) nuts about something/ someone (to be) ____

14) good egg (a) ____

15) low hanging fruit ____

16) play by the book (to) ____

17) due diligence ____

18) It is all Greek to me. (S) ____

19) keep one's shirt on (to) ____

20) stuffed shirt (a) ____

**B**

A)  to get along very well

B)  ex lover

C)  to throw cold water on

D)  to be ripped off/cheated

E)  the basics/fundamentals

F)  a good person

G)  opportunities that can be readily obtained

H)  to follow the rules/law

I)  investigation of facts before signing a contract

J)  I have no idea.

K)  to settle down/relax/be patient

L)  a buttoned-down person who believes he/she is superior

M)  to be suitable; to match

N)  to be ready

O)  to take extreme risks

P)  to move from a bad position to one that is worse

Q)  the $64,000.00 question

R)  a problem difficult to solve/fix

S)  to be crazy about

T)  to leave

## 17.E ➜ Writing Practice

**Task** ➜ Write a sentence using each idiom.

1) bend one's ear (to)

_____

2) take off (to)

_____

3) set up shop (in) (to)

_____

4) fire on all cylinders (to)

_____

5) play with fire (to)

_____

6) It is all Greek to me. (S)

_____

7) play by the book (to)

_____

8) hard nut to crack (a)

_____

9) corporation (a)

_____

10) in a nutshell

_____

11)  the upside is...

_____

12)  lose one's shirt (to)

_____

13)  due diligence

_____

14)  fit the bill (to)

_____

15)  burning question (the)

_____

## 17.F ➜ More Writing Practice

**<u>Task</u>** ➜ Write a short passage using as many idioms as you can from this lesson. The topic is your choice. Make it business-related if possible.

_____

_____

_____

_____

_____

_____

_____

_____

_____

# Lesson #18 ➜ *From the Ground Up*

➜ **5:00 p.m.** Maria shows Talita into the conference room.

✳ ✳ ✳

Talita: I was just getting on the train when you called.

Maria: Thanks for coming back at such short notice. I see from your résumé that you're from Sao Paulo. What is your visa status, if you don't mind my asking?

Talita: I have <u>a green card</u>. I won <u>the lottery</u> three years ago. So what's this all about? Why did I get <u>a call back</u>?

Maria: Let me <u>cut to the chase</u>. Austen Advertising is expanding. We're moving to a new office on Madison Avenue and I need an executive assistant. Does the position interest you? It would be full-time with benefits.

Talita: You want me to be your secretary? Sorry, but that's not what I had in mind. My skill set is on the creative side.

Maria: The job <u>entails</u> more than just <u>pushing paper</u>. As my assistant, you will have to travel with me throughout Latin America. Are you willing to travel?

Talita: Sure. I love traveling.

Maria: Good. Once you learn how <u>to navigate the system</u>, I will give you more responsibility. For example, if I can't go to Rio or Bogota to meet with a client, then you will have <u>to go in my stead</u>. If I can't attend meetings here, you will have to stand in for me and speak for our department.

Talita: You mean work with Joan Austen?

Maria: Yes. Ms. Austen is very demanding. She is not <u>a slave driver</u>, however, she doesn't suffer fools lightly. If your work is not <u>up to scratch</u>, she will <u>jump all over you</u>. She didn't get to the top <u>riding on someone else's coattails</u>. But if you <u>put your nose to the grindstone</u>, the sky's the limit.

Talita: I'd love to work with Ms. Austen. I bet she wears Prada.*

Maria: Prada? Never. Ms. Austen is very <u>down-to-earth</u>. Now I know this is not the position you wanted. However, there is no better way to learn the advertising business than <u>from the ground up</u>.

*\* See Movie-TV quotes pg. 214*

## 18.A → Definitions

1) *green card (a)*
   - in the U.S., a permanent-resident card which allows one to work legally
   _____
   _____

2) *lottery (the green card)*
   - the Diversity Immigrant Visa Lottery; U.S. government lottery that awards 50,000 green cards annually
   _____
   _____

3) *call back (a)*
   - a phone call inviting a prospective candidate to return for an interview
   _____
   _____

4) *cut to the chase (to)*
   - to state the bottom line
   _____
   _____

5) *entail (to)*
   - to include/involve
   _____
   _____

6) *pushing paper (to be)*
   - to be doing routine office work
   _____
   _____

7) *navigate the system (to)*
   - to know how to work within a system; to know the ropes
   _____
   _____

8) *go in one's stead (to)*
   - to substitute/stand in for
   _____
   _____

9) *slave driver (a)*
   - a superior with no compassion; dictator
   _____
   _____

10) *up to scratch (to be)*
   - to be done properly as required
   _____
   _____

11) *jump all over someone (to)*
   - to confront/attack without warning
   _____
   _____

12) *ride on one's coattails (to)*
   - to succeed not by ability but through connections
   _____
   _____

13) *put one's nose to the grindstone (to)*
   - to work hard
   _____
   _____

14) *down-to-earth (to be)*
   - to lack pretension; practical
   _____
   _____

15) *from the ground up*
   - from the lowest level up
   _____
   _____

## 18.B → Practice

__Task__ → Fill in the blanks using the idioms on the previous page.

1. The scuttlebutt is Ray, who is always blowing his horn, quickly climbed the corporate ladder by _____ his uncle Phil's _____ .

2. You took the words right out of my mouth. Patti is so _____ .

3. Let me _____ . You don't get a second chance to make a first impression.

4. Some of my coworkers are quite happy _____ all day. Not me. One of these days I'm going to be an A-player calling the shots.

5. This job _____ taking the red-eye to Boston once a week. Why so much travel? Because spending face-time with clients is important.

6. Dave's work hasn't _____ lately. He's not dotting his i's or crossing his t's. Personally, I think he's about to jump ship.

7. My boss is such _____ . Every morning she gives me my marching orders and says, "You know the drill. Don't drop the ball."

8. Al's skill set got his foot in the door. Now he's waiting for _____ .

9. We need to face the music and bring in new blood _____ .

10. It's time to roll up our sleeves and _____ .

11. Mary, I'm swamped. Can you _____ to that conference _____ ?

12. Tom _____ Cindy when she said that this company was nothing more than a stodgy old boys' club in need of an overhaul.

13. Here's the deal. You can't work legally in the U.S. without _____ .

14. Before you sign up for the Diversity Immigrant Visa _____ , make sure your hands are clean. If you win a green card, before you get it, U.S. immigration will go over your personal history with a fine-tooth comb.

15. You really need to buckle down and learn how _____ the new computer _____ . We have a lot riding on it.

## 18.C → The Story Continues

**Task** → Read the rest of the conversation, then answer the questions.

Maria: In a year or two, if all goes as planned, you'll be responsible for your own accounts. However, you are not finished school yet. You have one more year. So, what do you think? Would you like to sleep on it?

Talita: Are you kidding? I'm psyched. Totally. I accept. You know what they say: you snooze, you lose.

Maria: In that case, Ms. Alves, congratulations. Welcome to Austen Advertising. Come by tomorrow morning and we can get the ball rolling.

Talita: Great. By the way, what are the benefits?

Maria: You get complete dental and medical. Each has a two-hundred-and-fifty-dollar deductible. You can also enroll in a 401K.

Talita: Sweet. One more thing. Where's my office?

Maria: Sorry. No office. Just a cubicle. Is that a problem?

Talita: No. I'm just happy I've got a job. Thanks again. See you tomorrow.

Maria: Eight o'clock on the dot.

Talita: I'll be here. Bye.

## Questions

1. How many idioms can you identify in the passage above? What does each mean? Compare your choices to those on pg. 182. For definitions, see the word list, pg. 188.

2. Right time, right place. Explain how this phrase applies to Talita's getting a job at Austen Advertising. Was Talita lucky or did she make her own luck? Explain.

3. If you were in Talita's shoes, would you make the same choice? Explain.

4. In your country, is finishing college as important as it was in the past? What about in the United States? Explain.

5. Verbally summarize this lesson. Time yourself. You have <u>2</u> minutes.

## 18.D → Expansion

**Task** → Match the expressions in column A with the definitions in column B.

| A | B |
|---|---|
| 1) on cloud nine (to be) ____ | A) to make something more appealing than it actually is |
| 2) have a nose for something (to) ____ | B) excessive official rules limiting/stopping progress |
| 3) right under one's nose (to be) ____ | C) a note pad |
| 4) sugar coat (to) ____ | D) money |
| 5) brush up on something (to) ____ | E) to feel fantastic |
| 6) beat the system (to) ____ | F) to work at continually with slow progress |
| 7) red tape ____ | G) to go to the extreme |
| 8) taskmaster (a) ____ | H) What is going on? What are you doing? |
| 9) slave over something (to) ____ | I) the best; a paragon |
| 10) slave to something (to be a) ___ | J) to work in theory |
| 11) go to the ends of the earth (to) ____ | K) to review |
| 12) salt of the earth (the) ____ | L) to be so close you cannot see it |
| 13) What on earth? ____ | M) to disappear/vanish |
| 14) fall off the face of the earth (to) ____ | N) to have a talent or knack for |
| 15) the be-all and the end-all (S) ___ | O) to gain by breaking or bending the rules |
| 16) look good on paper (to) ____ | P) a slave driver |
| 17) paper over (to) ____ | Q) to have a strong desire for; addicted |
| 18) paper tiger (a) ____ | R) one who is ethical/down-to-earth |
| 19) scratch pad (a) ____ | S) to hide/cover up |
| 20) scratch ____ | T) to appear strong when weak in fact |

## 18.E → Writing Practice

**Task** → Write a sentence using each idiom.

1) sugarcoat (to)

_____

2) cut to the chase (to)

_____

3) red tape

_____

4) paper over (to)

_____

5) navigate the system (to)

_____

6) have a nose for something (to)

_____

7) the be-all and the end-all (S)

_____

8) up to scratch (to be)

_____

9) put one's nose to the grindstone (to)

_____

10) from the ground up

_____

11) beat the system (to)

_____

12) look good on paper (to)

_____

13) slave over something (to)

_____

14) pushing paper (to be)

_____

15) ride on one's coattails (to)

_____

## 18.F ➜ More Writing Practice

**Task** ➜ Write a short passage using as many idioms as you can from this lesson. The topic is your choice. Make it business-related if possible.

_____

_____

_____

_____

_____

_____

_____

_____

_____

# Lesson #19 ➜ *Crossing the Rubicon*

➜ **5:45 p.m.** Joan and Maria enter the new office on Madison Avenue.

**✽ ✽ ✽**

Joan:     Once I got over the <u>sticker shock</u>, I knew this was the place. So? What do you think?

Maria:     What do I think? "<u>Toto, I have a feeling we're not in Kansas anymore</u>." *

Joan:     Location, location, location, right?

Maria:     Right. Like you said, "Image is everything." And this place definitely <u>sends the right vibe</u>. I love the windows and the natural light. Very organic.

Joan:     This building is completely <u>eco-friendly</u>. The wood paneling is recycled milk cartons and the floor is recycled tires.

Maria:     Amazing. Were you able <u>to cut a deal with the building owner</u>?

Joan:     Yes. She said she'd <u>throw in the utilities</u> if I'd sign a ten-year lease.

Maria:     You signed a ten-year lease?

Joan:     Yes. Why?

Maria:     I'd say we just <u>crossed the Rubicon</u>.

Joan:     What's wrong? You <u>look as nervous as a cat in a room full of rocking chairs</u>.

Maria:     I'm not nervous. I'm just <u>itching to move</u>, that's all.

Joan:     Me too. This place just felt right. I know I should've shopped around, but I'm like you. I know it when I see it.

Maria:     You deserve <u>a pat on the back</u>. Serious. Lots of people can <u>talk the talk, but they can't walk the walk</u>. Not you. You have all the talent in the world.

Joan:     Talent has nothing to do with it. Like Edison said, "Genius is one percent inspiration and ninety-nine percent perspiration." Anyway, cash wise, we might <u>feel the pinch</u> for a while, what with the move and the recent hires, but we'll <u>weather the storm</u>.

Maria:     I heard you <u>hooked Jane Frost</u>. How did you <u>swing that</u>?

       *\* See Movie-TV quotes pg. 214*

## 19.A → Definitions

1) *sticker shock*
   - the shock received from the high price on a sales tag

2) *Toto, I have a feeling we're not in Kansas anymore.*
   - The realization that you have entered a strange new world.

3) *send the right /wrong vibe (to)*
   - to send the right/wrong message

4) *eco-friendly (to be)*
   - to be good for the environment

5) *cut a deal with someone (to)*
   - to seal the deal

6) *throw in something (to)*
   - to include at no extra cost

7) *cross the Rubicon (to)*
   - to cross the point of no return

8) *look as nervous as a cat in a room full of rocking chairs (to)*
   - to look nervous/scared/anxious

9) *itching to (do something) (to be)*
   - to be impatiently waiting to proceed

10) *pat on the back (a)*
    - congratulations/kudos

11) *talk the talk and walk the walk (to)*
    - the ability to put words into action

12) *feel the pinch (to)*
    - to feel the restricting effects of cost cutting

13) *weather the storm (to)*
    - to survive a difficult time

14) *hook someone/something (to)*
    - to get/obtain

15) *swing something (to)*
    - to manage/achieve/resolve

## 19.B → Practice

**Task** → Fill in the blanks using the idioms on the previous page.

1.  Uri in marketing deserves a big _____
    for finally getting the show on the road.

2.  Aya is just _____ put the pedal to the metal and seal the deal.

3.  Suffice it to say, a laptop is not _____ . Why not? Let's cut to the
    chase. A laptop, from making to recycling, produces 350 kg of C02, which is
    comparable to 240 liters of orange juice.

4.  We haven't _____ with Apple per se. As I said, we
    are still just talking. Hopefully, an LOI is right around the corner.

5.  Be prepared for _____ when you look for houses in
    this neck of the woods. It is definitely upscale.

6.  Ahmad sure can _____ , but when push
    comes to shove, he sure can't _____ .

7.  Do not hire that man. He's _____ .
    It's obvious that he's trying to pull the wool over our eyes.

8.  No more coffee or tea? This company is really _____ .

9.  Even though Alok is a slave driver, I always manage _____ ,
    like water off a duck's back.

10. When I arrived in Tokyo for the first time, I looked around and said, " _____
    _____ ."

11. You got a twenty-percent raise? How did you _____ that?

12. You have a nice house, but your roof is not up to scratch. Here's the deal. I
    will buy your house if you _____ a new roof.

13. If you are in a Catch-22, no matter which way you choose, you will end up
    _____ .

14. Francesco _____ .
    If he doesn't get a call back, he's going to be pounding the pavement again.

15. Markuss would love _____ a green card. His dream is to
    set up shop in America. He hates his current job. Pushing paper all day for a
    big corporation is not his cup of tea.

## 19.C ➜ The Story Continues

**Task** ➜ Read the rest of the conversation, then answer the questions.

Joan:     How did I hook Ms. Jane Frost? Simple. I told her there's no glass ceiling at Austen Advertising. Also, she's agreed to head up our London office. She's from London, so she jumped at the chance.

Maria:    I've heard she can be a handful.

Joan:     It comes with the territory. You want the best? You get the best, and everything else that comes with it. But think about it: when the deal is on the line, when you are fighting for every slice of the pie, who do you want in your corner? A poodle or a shark?

Maria:    Have you announced it?

Joan:     No. I'll send out a memo after we move in. But for now, Mum's the word on Ms. Frost. Have you seen your new office? Come. Have a look. Well? What do you think?

Maria:    A corner office? Oh, my god!

## Questions

1. How many idioms can you identify in the passage above? What does each mean? Compare your choices to those on pg. 184. For definitions, see the word list, pg. 188.

2. Who is Jane Frost? Why has she entered the picture? Why is she a hand full? Explain.

3. Why did Ms. Frost decide to work for Austen Advertising? Explain.

4. Have you ever crossed the Rubicon? What is the origin of this idiom? Explain.

5. Verbally summarize this lesson. Time yourself. You have <u>2</u> minutes.

## 19.D → Expansion

**Task** → Match the expressions in column A with the definitions in column B.

**A**

**B**

1) All the world's a stage. (S) ____

2) in the loop (to be) ____

3) sit on the fence (to) ____

4) size up (to) ____

5) critical mass ____

6) cut off one's nose to spite one's face (to) ____

7) cut-and-dry (to be) ____

8) have buyer's remorse (to) ____

9) in a pinch (to be) ____

10) throw one's hat in the ring (to) ____

11) talk through one's hat (to) ____

12) move the goal posts (to) ____

13) tough putt (a) ____

14) slam-dunk (a) ____

15) crash course (a) ____

16) homestretch (the) ____

17) whole nine yards (the) ____

18) even playing field (an) ____

19) in the pipeline (to be) ____

20) margin of error (the) ____

A) to be in the circle of communication; connected

B) an intensive course in which much is learned in little or no time

C) the final part/phase of a project

D) when the competition is equally matched

E) to be in the development process

F) the amount of allowable error

G) a difficult golf shot; a challenge

H) to inspect in detail

I) to fail to see the negative consequences of one's actions

J) to be straightforward/clear

K) to be in a situation in which a substitute is the only alternative

L) the minimum amount to start/maintain a business/process

M) to enter/join

N) to sound like an expert when one is not

O) the arbitrary changing of rules often to serve a losing side

P) a sure thing

Q) to make no decision either way

R) Life is theater and we are all actors.

S) everything; from soup to nuts

T) to regret buying something

## 19.E ➔ Writing Practice

**Task** ➔ Write a sentence using each idiom.

1)   cross the Rubicon (to)

_____

2)   All the world's a stage. (S)

_____

3)   crash course (a)

_____

4)   move the goal posts (to)

_____

5)   itching to (do something) (to be)

_____

6)   feel the pinch (to)

_____

7)   cut a deal with someone (to)

_____

8)   have buyer's remorse (to)

_____

9)   sticker shock

_____

10)   send the right vibe (to)

_____

11) eco-friendly (to be)

_____

12) slam-dunk (a)

_____

13) whole nine yards (the)

_____

14) in a pinch (to be)

_____

15) weather the storm (to)

_____

## 19.F ➜ More Writing Practice

**Task** ➜ Write a short passage using as many idioms as you can from this lesson. The topic is your choice. Make it business-related if possible.

_____

_____

_____

_____

_____

_____

_____

_____

# Lesson #20 ➜ *All's Well That Ends Well*

➜ **8:00 p.m.** The Waldorf-Astoria. Joan meets Maria outside a dining room.

❋ ❋ ❋

Joan:    Well look at you. You'll have them eating out of your hand.

Maria:   Joan, what am I doing here? I <u>feel like a fish out of water</u>. Look at these people. This is <u>a who's who of Manhattan</u>. I could've sworn I saw Bill Clinton. I'm so out of my league. I want <u>to crawl inside a hole and die</u>.

Joan:    Later. You've got work to do. As the new head of our Latin American division, I want you <u>to work the room</u> and give me <u>a run-down</u> tomorrow. I suggest you start with David Hamilton. He's entering now. See? He's the marketing director for American Aerospace. If we sign A.A., we will be <u>sitting pretty</u>. Maria? <u>Earth to Maria</u>. Hel-lo?

Maria:   He's so handsome.

Joan:    He just got divorced—and he's <u>rolling in it</u>.

Maria:   Really? Well, that changes everything.

Joan:    Got your cards?

Maria:   Oh, yeah. I think I'll <u>powder my nose</u> first. Where's <u>the little girl's room</u>?

Joan:    Down the hall on the left. Remember. These suits are our <u>bread-and-butter</u>. Not only that but at this level, it is a very small world. <u>The grapevine</u> is alive and well. What you do and say will be all over town tomorrow.

Maria:   So what are you saying?

Joan:    I'm saying, <u>keep your eye on the prize</u> no matter how beautiful the scenery.

Maria:   <u>Keep it on the up-and-up</u>. Right. Got it. So where's the guest-of-honor, your husband?

Joan:    My what?

Maria:   Don. Your husband. Don't look at me like that. He called yesterday to say that he'd had your engagement ring resized.

Joan:    So <u>the cat is out of the bag</u>.

Maria:   Congratulations.

Joan:    Thanks. You have your marching orders. Now go bang the drum.

## 20.A → Definitions

1) *feel like a fish out of water (to)*
   - to feel lost/out of place

2) *who's who of something/somewhere (a)*
   - the best of the best from...

3) *crawl inside a hole and die (to)*
   - to hide due to embarrassment

4) *work the (a) room (to)*
   - to schmooze

5) *run-down (a)*
   - a report/update

6) *sitting pretty (to be)*
   - to be in an advantageous position

7) *Earth to someone.*
   - Hello? Are you awake/paying attention?

8) *rolling in it (to be)*
   - to be rolling in money; rich/wealthy

9) *powder one's nose (to)*
   - to freshen up in the women's restroom

10) *little girl's/boy's room (the)*
    - the women's/men's restroom

11) *bread-and-butter (to be one's)*
    - to be one's main source of income

12) *grapevine (the)*
    - the rumor mill

13) *keep one's eye on the prize (to)*
    - to stay focused on one's goal

14) *keep it on the up-and-up (to)*
    - to be professional/ethical

15) *cat is out of the bag (the)*
    - the secret is out

## 20.B → Practice

**Task** → Fill in the blanks using the idioms on the previous page.

1.  When Ali stepped off the plane at JFK for the first time, he had no time _____ . He had to hit the ground running and meet a client.

2.  Yasemin is _____ . Why? Because she always puts her nose to the grindstone and is never afraid to go out on a limb and up the ante.

3.  I've heard through _____ that Adam would throw his own grandmother under the bus to seal that deal.

4.  Alok is definitely _____ . It's a seller's market and his house has curb appeal and, best of all, location, location, location.

5.  Lars loves _____ . He says it's good for his ego.

6.  Good morning, everybody. This _____ on the new database will be brief. Suffice it to say, I'm still learning how to navigate it.

7.  Have you seen the attendee list? It's _____ of the film industry. Bear in mind, though, the conference fee is through the roof.

8.  When Onur learned that his company had been cutting corners for years, he wanted _____ .

9.  Look at him. Asleep at the wheel again. _____ to Richard. Hel-lo? We are leaving. Hel-lo?

10. Pitching over the phone is a tough putt, I know. The trick is to state the bottom line from the get-go and always _____ .

11. Mark was always telling me _____ when he was the one caught red-handed stealing pens from the store room.

12. There's a big difference between _____ and taking a powder. The latter means "chilling" while the former means freshening up.

13. Excuse me? Can you tell me where _____ is?

14. _____ . Yes, I did indeed win a green card.

15. Writing ESL text books is his _____ . One day, he will publish a novel, but until then he will continue to write for his niche market.

## 20.C ➜ The Story Continues

**Task** ➜ Read the rest of the conversation, then answer the questions.

*(Don crosses the lobby of the Waldorf and approaches Joan.)*

Joan:   So is it official? Is your name on the shingle?

Don:   It is. They've also given me two weeks off. How does Tahiti sound?

Joan:   Tahiti sounds divine, but...

Don:   Hawaii? I could teach you how to surf.

Joan:   You know I'm transitioning into a new space.

Don:   Pizza and a movie?

Joan:   Stop.

Don:   So what should I do?

Joan:   Take a rain check?

Don:   The story of my life. C'mon. They're serving dinner. I ordered you vegan.

Joan:   Great. I'm starved.

Don:   You know what?

Joan:   What?

Don:   I think this is the beginning of a beautiful friendship.*

*(They enter the dining room, arm in arm.)*

## Questions

1. How many idioms can you identify in the passage above? What does each mean? Compare your choices to those on pg. 185. For definitions, see the word list, pg. 188.

2. Why can't Joan go away? Explain.

3. Do you think Joan will change her last name when she gets married? Why? Why not? What would you do if you were Joan? Explain.

4. Look into the future. Summarize Joan's life five and ten years from now.

5. Verbally summarize this lesson. Time yourself. You have <u>2</u> minutes.

   * See Movie-TV quotes pg. 214

## 20.D ➜ Expansion

**Task** ➜ Match the expressions in column A with the definitions in column B.

**A**

1) have a grasp of something (to) ____

2) prospects ____

3) work-life balance ____

4) pitfall (a) ____

5) sit in the catbird seat (to) ____

6) bread-winner (the) ____

7) nest egg (a) ____

8) tasked with (to be) ____

9) up-and-comer (an) ____

10) play favorites (to) ____

11) earn one's stripes (to) ____

12) boondoggle (a) ____

13) have a thick skin (to) ____

14) have zero tolerance for something (to) ____

15) promote from within (to) ____

16) Don't look a gift horse in the mouth. ____

17) make a splash (to) ____

18) scale back one's hours (to) ____

19) take a calculated risk (to) ____

20) All's well that ends well. (S) ____

**B**

A) everything is fine; no problem

B) chances of success

C) one who brings money home

D) to be assigned to

E) to understand the task/issue

F) a problem, potential or actual

G) a waste of time and money

H) one with excellent future prospects

I) to be tough/resilient/resolute

J) to promote in-house employees

K) to reduce one's working hours

L) to risk after assessing the odds

M) the balance between work and family life

N) to make a favorable impression

O) Don't question the quality of a gift.

P) to have no room for unethical behavior

Q) to demonstrate competency

R) to show preference/bias

S) long-term personal retirement savings

T) to be sitting pretty

## 20.E → Writing Practice

**Task** → Write a sentence using each idiom.

1) feel like a fish out of water (to)

_____

2) tasked with (to be)

_____

3) who's who of something (a)

_____

4) run-down (a)

_____

5) grapevine (the)

_____

6) have a thick skin (to)

_____

7) nest egg

_____

8) play favorites (to)

_____

9) keep one's eye on the prize (to)

_____

10) keep it on the up-and-up (to)

_____

11) bread-winner (the)

_____

12) have zero tolerance for something (to)

_____

13) earn one's stripes (to)

_____

14) prospects

_____

15) take a calculated risk (to)

_____

## 20.F ➜ More Writing Practice

**Task** ➜ Write a short passage using as many idioms as you can from this
lesson. The topic is your choice. Make it business-related if possible.

_____

_____

_____

_____

_____

_____

_____

_____

_____

## Review #5

**Task** ➜ Fill in the blanks using the following idioms.

| | | |
|---|---|---|
| 1. down-to-earth | 10. fits the bill | 19. prospects |
| 2. a pat on the back | 11. boondoggles | 20. red tape |
| 3. calculated risk | 12. itching to | 21. up-and-comer |
| 4. a thick skin | 13. set up shop | 22. cut a deal with |
| 5. an even playing field | 14. taskmaster | 23. earn your stripes |
| 6. a call back | 15. move the goal posts | 24. from the ground up |
| 7. eco-friendly | 16. work-life balance | 25. beat the system |
| 8. zero tolerance for | 17. make a splash | 26. scale back one's hours |
| 9. play by the book | 18. margin of error | 27. keep it on the up-and-up |

1.  I think we should give Ian _____ . He _____
    _____ and seems like a _____ guy.

2.  When there is a lot of _____ , it is hard to _____ .
    In that case, you just have to _____ .

3.  Management has _____    _____ .
    When you attend that conference in Vegas, remember to _____
    _____ or else you will get your walking papers.

4.  I really need to _____ my _____ and reassess my
    _____    _____ .

5.  Mick deserves _____ for _____
    Coca Cola. Mick is a real _____ . Keep your eye on him.

6.  The company intends to _____ by _____ in every major city
    in the U.S. It is a _____ but the _____ look good.

7.  You have to have _____ working with Mike. He is such a
    _____ . You really have to _____ .

8.  Margaret is just _____ pitch _____ products.

9.  This market is not an _____ . The government keeps
    _____ for the benefit of domestic producers.

10. In business, the _____ is very small, indeed.

# Answer Key

## Lesson #1 ➜ *Stuck in Traffic* ➜ pg. 11

### 1.B - Practice - pg. 13

1. Bob got up early because he wanted **to beat the traffic (2)**.

2. When you are **stuck in traffic (1)**, you have no choice but to sit and wait it out.

3. Al is **not a happy camper (11)**. He just learned that he is going to be let go.

4. After Joan and Alexander **sealed the deal (6)**, they celebrated with dinner and a Broadway show.

5. Yurica is always **going to bat for (8)** the homeless.

6. When people slow down **to rubberneck (3)**, they often cause fender benders.

7. When Carol ordered a hamburger, she told the server **to hold (15)** the onions.

8. To meet the deadline, the team had **to pull out all the stops (9)**.

9. Maria never fails **to bring** a project **in under budget (10)**.

10. Joan wanted Rick **to work up (12)** a new slogan by tomorrow.

11. Carla has arranged to have **a working lunch (14)** with the new client.

12. After the prototype failed, the team had **to go back to the drawing board (13)**.

13. In business, making a profit is **the bottom line (5)**.

14. Bob's last idea was terrible, but this time he **hit it out of the park (7)**.

15. Steve told the lazy intern **to put a fire under it (4)**.

### 1.C - The Story Continues - pg. 14

Maria: Anything else, Joan?
Joan: Nothing for now. I'll see you when I get in.
Maria: Have you thought about what we talked about?
Joan: Thought about what?
Maria: You know, my raise.
Joan: Right. Sorry, I <u>have so much on my plate</u>, it <u>slipped my mind</u>.
Maria: You said I'm <u>in line for one</u>.
Joan: I did. But we're <u>facing a budget crunch</u>. The move to a bigger office is going <u>to eat into our cash flow</u>.
Maria: So that means no raise?
Joan: Not necessarily. Let's <u>circle back to it</u> when I get in, okay?

## 1.D - Expansion - pg. 15

| | | | |
|---|---|---|---|
| 1. T | 6. C | 11. E | 16. M |
| 2. A | 7. P | 12. O | 17. G |
| 3. S | 8. Q | 13. F | 18. L |
| 4. R | 9. D | 14. N | 19. H |
| 5. B | 10. I | 15. K | 20. J |

# Lesson #2 ➜ A Rain Check ➜ pg. 18

## 2.B - Practice - pg. 20

1. Anne is **in the market for** (8) a new house.

2. Apple had **to ramp up** (10) production to meet the Christmas demand.

3. **In this neck of the woods** (13), you'll always get stuck in traffic.

4. Before you seal a deal, you had better **run the numbers** (15) first.

5. **The scuttlebutt** (11) is the boss is not a happy camper.

6. Don pulled out all the stops to get his name on **the shingle** (2).

7. The bottom line is our cash flow is **through the roof** (14).

8. The auditors are coming? Really? Thanks for **the heads up** (12).

9. Adriana had **to burn the midnight oil** (7) to meet the morning deadline.

10. In Hollywood, Stephen Spielberg is definitely **a heavy hitter** (4).

11. This subway system is so old, it is **bursting at the seams** (9).

12. Linda is such **a schmoozer** (6). She'll do anything to seal the deal.

13. Frank loves **to rub elbows with** (3) heavy hitters.

14. Jason got a raise and a promotion. He really hit it out of the park this time. The **icing on the cake** (1) is his new corner office.

15. I can't make the working lunch, sorry. I'll have to **take a rain check** (5)

## 2.C - The Story Continues - pg. 21

Don: Just for the record, the party starts at eight.
Joan: How can I turn a profit if I'm always out tripping the light fantastic?
Don: An evening away from work is not going to sink the ship.
Joan: I don't know. I need incentive. Make me an offer.
Don: Consider it a tax write off.

Joan:   Taxes? Bor-ing. Can't you <u>sweeten the deal</u>?
Don:    All right. Marry me.
Joan:   Marry you? Hmmm. Interesting. <u>Is that your final offer</u>?*
Don:    I'll tell you tonight. Bye.

*(Don exits from the elevator.)*

## 2.D - Expansion - pg. 22

| | | | | | | | |
|---|---|---|---|---|---|---|---|
| 1. | E | 6. | I | 11. | H | 16. | T |
| 2. | A | 7. | F | 12. | R | 17. | M |
| 3. | J | 8. | K | 13. | Q | 18. | B |
| 4. | N | 9. | L | 14. | D | 19. | G |
| 5. | S | 10. | C | 15. | P | 20. | O |

## Lesson #3 ➔ *An In* ➔ pg. 25

### 3.B - Practice - pg. 27

1.  I've heard that movie is **a** real **dog (1)**.

2.  Google is **the 800-pound gorilla (3)** in the internet-search business.

3.  Elvia **jumped ship (10)** because she got a better offer.

4.  Talita would love **to land (12)** a job at Austen Advertising.

5.  The company intends **to clean house (5)**? Really? No, I hadn't heard. Thanks for the heads up.

6.  We are losing market share. Our competitors are **eating our lunch (2)**.

7.  The scuttlebutt is the CEO has **gone off the rails (4)**.

8.  Now that we've sealed the deal, **the sky is the limit (13)**.

9.  Don't worry. I **have got it covered (7)** I just ran the numbers.

10. What do we **stand to gain (9)** if we hire a heavy hitter?

11. The company is in the market for some **new blood (6)**.

12. These **back-of-the-envelope calculations (11)** are through the roof.

13. Joe is such a schmoozer. I swear, he **has an in (8)** everywhere.

14. Joan is **having kittens (14)** because we forgot to work up some ideas.

15. "Why does Anne **look like the cat that ate the canary (15)**?" Brian asked. "Because," Dave replied, "she brought the project in under budget."

## 3.C - The Story Continues - pg. 28

Judy: Great news. I'm having lunch with John Phillips, GM's V.P. of marketing. The buzz is GM is leaving Art Advertising and Mr. Phillips wants to be, and I quote, "Brought up to speed on Austen Advertising."
Joan: That's fantastic.
Judy: Nothing is set in stone. This little tête-à-tête is just a trial balloon.
Joan: It doesn't matter. Pull out all the stops.
Judy: Believe me, I'm going to make him an offer he can't refuse.*
Joan: Where are you taking him?
Judy: He's taking me to that new French place, La Baguette. Have you been?
Joan: No. I'm off butter and cream.
Judy: Me too. But I'm willing to take one for the team if it means snagging GM.

## 3.D - Expansion - pg. 29

| 1. | M | 6. | A | 11. | B | 16. | S |
| 2. | F | 7. | I | 12. | L | 17. | E |
| 3. | C | 8. | R | 13. | J | 18. | K |
| 4. | N | 9. | T | 14. | Q | 19. | G |
| 5. | O | 10. | P | 15. | D | 20. | H |

# Lesson #4 ➜ A Bump in the Road ➜ pg. 32

## 4.B - Practice - pg. 34

1. The iPhone, the Big Mac and Diet Coke are all **cash cows (15)**.

2. Jake wants to shoot a TV commercial on Mt. Everest. Joan, however, **threw cold water on (5)** that idea and told him to go back to the drawing board.

3. To seal the deal, the team really has **to step up to the plate (13)**.

4. Joan hired Sylvia because she always **thinks outside the box (7)**. The woman is bursting at the seams with ideas.

5. Josh is always late. The scuttlebutt is his head is **on the chopping block (9)**.

6. When a politician says, "It's time to clean house!" you know she is **talking out of both sides of her mouth (4)**.

7. During their working lunch, Joan **fleshed out (10)** some new ideas for a new client, a heavy hitter on Wall Street.

8. Before you run the numbers, I want you **to run** that idea **by me (11)** before I give you the OK.

9. Don't worry about the Christmas party. It's only September. We'll **cross that bridge when we come to it (12)**.

10. Ewa speaks English perfectly, yet she is always **selling herself short** (14).

11. The team really **bent over backwards** (6) to make the client happy.

12. Stop **flip-flopping** (8). Put a fire under it and hit one out of the park.

13. If someone says, "Just give me **the gist** (3)," she means, "I don't have time for the whole story. Just give me the bottom line."

14. I see you're not eating sushi. **I take it that** (1) you don't like Japanese food.

15. If you want the best deals on **Black Friday** (2), you had better not get stuck in traffic. By 5:00 a.m., retail stores are already bursting at the seams with customers.

## 4.C - The Story Continues - pg. 35

Joan:     Right. Moving on. How's Bobcat Beer doing? What's the latest?
Jake:     Steve is giving the owner the pitch at the brewery this morning.
Joan:     Good. How is the new man Steve doing?
Jake:     I had my doubts at first, but he's really pulled up his socks. As you know, he signed Office Station last week. They loved his pitch. I'm telling you, the guy is a natural. He hits all the right notes. We definitely lucked out when we landed him.
Joan:     That's good to hear. What about Bobcat Beer? Does it look like a done deal?
Jake:     I'll go out on a limb and say yes. Steve is a closer. He will get the account. In the meantime, keep your fingers crossed.

## 4.D - Expansion - pg. 36

| | | | | | | | |
|---|---|---|---|---|---|---|---|
| 1. | T | 6. | O | 11. | Q | 16. | I |
| 2. | M | 7. | B | 12. | R | 17. | G |
| 3. | N | 8. | C | 13. | F | 18. | H |
| 4. | A | 9. | L | 14. | J | 19. | E |
| 5. | D | 10. | P | 15. | S | 20. | K |

## Review #1 ➔ Pg. 39

1. The **bottom line** (11) is you need to **pull out all the stops** (2) if you want to **seal the deal** (16).

2. According to my **back-of-the-envelope calculations** (26), we **stand to gain** (27) if we bring in **new blood** (1) and **ramp up** (25) production.

3. **In this neck of the woods** (20), very few people are **in the market for** (12) a single-family home. Most want apartments or condos.

4.  Camille **landed** (5) a job with IBM because she **had an in** (13). Her boyfriend is a **heavy hitter** (24) in the finance department. **The icing on the cake** (23) is she gets stock options.

5.  Daniela will not be **a happy camper** (9) if you don't **bring** this project **in under budget** (21).

6.  After Carolina **threw cold water on** (6) Hector's idea, he **went off the rails** (15). I'd avoid him. He's still **having kittens** (22).

7.  A **working lunch** (7) is not the time to **schmooze** (3). It is time to **hold** (4) the alcohol and **flesh out** (17) ideas.

8.  You often have to **bend over backwards** (19) when **thinking outside the box** (8).

9.  Tom gave Jill **the gist** (14) of what happened during the meeting.

10. If you want to **beat the traffic** (18), you'd better not **rubberneck** (10).

## Lesson #5 → *All the Rage* → pg. 40

### 5.B - Practice - pg. 42

1.  Because that product was such a dog, the company decided **to pull the plug** (11) and go back to the drawing board.

2.  A **trendsetter** (8) is someone who thinks outside the box.

3.  Retailers in the U.S. **have a lot riding on** (3) Black Friday.

4.  The bottom line is we've been **spinning our wheels** (7) for too long. It's time to step up to the plate and start thinking outside the box.

5.  I know you like working here, but this company is going out of business. Believe me, it's time **to face the music** (10) and start pounding the pavement for a new job.

6.  I prefer beer, thanks. Whiskey is **not my cup of tea** (15).

7.  "That client talks out of both sides of his mouth," Hector said. "**Ditto that** (14)," Maria replied.

8.  A lot of famous people take **the red-eye** (1) from L.A. to New York. If you take it, you never know with whom you might rub elbows.

9.  When I bought my laptop, I told the clerk to hold the **freebie** (6). I've already got three printers. I don't need another.

10. Dave called to say he loved the idea. He is definitely **on board** (2).

11. I take it you're working on the **tagline** (5) for Biagi Pizza, yes?

12. Last year, stretchy jeans were **all the rage** (4).

13. Michelle told Al to put a fire under it. He's been **resting on his laurels** (9) for too long.

14. Apple is eating Microsoft's lunch. That said, Microsoft needs to face the music and focus more on their **core competency** (12): software.

15. I can't believe it. Lady Gaga **sold out to** (13) Disney!

## 5.C - The Story Continues - pg. 43

Beth: So, Jake, how's it going?

Jake: I have got a lot on my plate, but I'm managing to keep my head above water. My wife just had a baby.

Beth: Congrats. Boy or girl?

Jake: A boy. James Andrew.

Beth: You must be so proud.

Jake: Yeah. And bagged. He sleeps all day and cries all night. I have definitely hit the wall. How about you? What's shaking in your world?

Beth: Nothing to write home about. Don't forget we have a working lunch. Mario Biagi is raising Cain.

Jake: Again? What's wrong this time?

Beth: That is the $64,000.00 question.

## 5.D - Expansion - pg. 44

| | | | | | | | |
|---|---|---|---|---|---|---|---|
| 1. | J | 6. | N | 11. | B | 16. | K |
| 2. | H | 7. | R | 12. | C | 17. | O |
| 3. | T | 8. | Q | 13. | I | 18. | S |
| 4. | P | 9. | G | 14. | D | 19. | L |
| 5. | M | 10. | A | 15. | E | 20. | F |

# Lesson #6 → A Pink Slip → pg. 47

## 6.B - Practice - pg. 49

1. If Rob gets stuck in traffic, he **goes ballistic** (8).

2. The accountant was arrested after he **dipped into** (1) a client's bank account.

3. Don't quote me but **rumor has it that** (2) the president will be here next week.

4. We have **given** Hal **enough rope** (13), and look what happens. He's still asleep at the wheel.

5. You **took the words right out of my mouth (15)**. I agree. It's time to clean house and bring in new blood.

6. Racism, sexism and **ageism (9)** are forms of work-place discrimination.

7. I gave it my best shot trying to seal the deal. **Let the chips fall where they may (12)**.

8. Carlos decided to pull the plug on **moonlighting (3)** as a pizza driver. He felt he was just spinning his wheels while burning the candle at both ends.

9. When I **caught** Bob **red-handed (4)** stealing my sandwich in the lunch room, he said he thought it was a freebie the client had sent over.

10. It's **high time (5)** we ran the numbers. We really need to see if our back-of-the envelope calculations are in the ball park or not.

11. After the president cheated on his wife, the press **dragged his name through the mud (10)**.

12. I just **got my walking papers (6)**. That's okay. No big deal. Working for this company never was my cup of tea anyway.

13. You want to sue Apple for not offering enough phone apps? What do I think? To be honest, you **don't have a leg to stand on (11)**.

14. As we entered the meeting, Bob whispered, "**Take no prisoners (14)**."

15. Years ago, if you got **a pink slip (7)**—a real pink piece of paper—you knew that your head was on the chopping block.

## 6.C - The Story Continues - pg. 50

Judy: All right. So enough about Cresten. What about you? When was the last time you took a vacation?
Joan: Vacation is not in my vocabulary.
Judy: Joan, you need a break. You're running yourself ragged.
Joan: I have a business to run. Besides, I'm that close to buying a place in Tribeca. A cozy-little pied-à-terre. All I have to do is sign on the dotted line, but I keep getting cold feet.
Judy Why? Too much?
Joan: No. The price is definitely doable. It's just that when people get older they usually retreat to the suburbs and don't come back. I am doing the exact opposite: going against the grain (S).
Judy: Hey, if you like the place, go for it. Remember what you always tell me? Your motto? No regrets. What does Don think? Are you two moving in? Did his divorce papers come through?
Joan: What is this? Twenty questions?
Judy: Just asking. (exiting) He's definitely a keeper.

## 6.D - Expansion - pg. 51

| | | | | | | | |
|---|---|---|---|---|---|---|---|
| 1. | C | 6. | D | 11. | N | 16. | P |
| 2. | B | 7. | G | 12. | K | 17. | A |
| 3. | O | 8. | H | 13. | S | 18. | R |
| 4. | F | 9. | L | 14. | M | 19. | T |
| 5. | E | 10. | J | 15. | I | 20. | Q |

## Lesson #7 ➜ *The Only Game in Town* ➜ pg. 54

### 7.B - Practice - pg. 56

1. Sally loves movies. She would **kill (11)** to work in Hollywood.

2. Harold is **a wiz at (14)** fixing computers.

3. If you want to swim with the sharks, you can't be afraid **to blow your own horn (13)**.

4. Sylvia had to cancel the working lunch because she was all **tied up (1)**.

5. Your **skill set (12)** describes your core competency.

6. When Charlie wheels and deals, he takes no prisoners. If you didn't know him, you would say he was **off his rocker (3)**.

7. In this neck of the woods, there are a lot of big-box stores. But for price and value, Wal-Mart is really **the only game in town (9)**.

8. Nigel tried to fix his car, but in the end he had to admit that he was not **cut out to be (7)** a mechanic.

9. Moonlighting is **a far cry from (5)** having a career.

10. Sara **followed in** her mother's **footsteps (6)** and became a dentist.

11. When you fly internationally, the only document that will **suffice (15)** for personal I.D. is a valid passport.

12. When Mariana retires, she wants **to hang her hat (8)** in Florida.

13. After applying to Goldman Sachs for many years, Berta finally **got her foot in the door (4)**.

14. As far as Tim is concerned, **no one can hold a candle to (10)** Google.

15. I've never met Paul, but rumor has it he's **a kick (2)**.

## 7.C - The Story Continues - pg. 57

Hector:  Who was that <u>all bright-eyed and bushy-tailed</u>?
Maria:  An intern applicant. She's quite <u>the name-dropper</u>.
Hector:  <u>It's not what you know, but who you know</u>, right?
Maria:  That's how you got this job.
Hector:  Okay, don't <u>rub it in</u>.
Maria:  And you still owe me. So when are you taking me out for dinner?
Hector:  Where do you want to go?
Maria:  How about that new French restaurant, La Baguette?
Hector:  That place? Forget it. It <u>costs an arm and a leg</u>. Besides, you practically <u>have to inherit a reservation</u>. How about pizza? Pizza, a couple of <u>brewskies</u> and <u>the Yanks</u> on TV. Oh, yeah. <u>Now we're talking</u>.
Maria:  You know what I like about you, Hector Gomez?
Hector:  What?
Maria:  *(exiting)* <u>You know how to treat a girl right</u>.

## 7.D - Expansion - pg. 58

| | | | | | | | |
|---|---|---|---|---|---|---|---|
| 1. | O | 6. | B | 11. | E | 16. | H |
| 2. | J | 7. | C | 12. | M | 17. | I |
| 3. | P | 8. | T | 13. | L | 18. | Q |
| 4. | A | 9. | N | 14. | D | 19. | K |
| 5. | S | 10. | F | 15. | G | 20. | R |

# Lesson #8 ➜ *The Pitch* ➜ pg. 61

## 8.B - Practice - pg. 63

1. To avoid the high cost of maintaining large **inventories (6)**, many publishers, large and small, are now print-on-demand (POD) only.

2. **Joe (1)** is not my cup of tea. Thanks, anyway.

3. We've been spinning our wheels for too long. It is time **to roll up our sleeves (11)** and get to work. We have a lot riding on this product.

4. **Let me lay it on the line (14)**. In this business, we take no prisoners.

5. **Revenue (2)** this year is a far cry from what it was last year. I suggest you run the numbers again just to double check.

6. Dave is so wishy-washy. For once, I wish he'd just **lay his cards on the table (3)**.

7. I don't know why the media is dragging his name through the mud. Don't they **have bigger fish to fry (13)**?

8.  Toni is really **raking in (8)** the money moonlighting as an estate planner.

9.  Sorry, but you don't really have the skill set to be a TV **pitchman (9)**.

10. Why did I go ballistic? Because that fender-bender **set me back (10)** five G's. I am not a happy camper, believe me.

11. We need to ramp up production. The orders are just **piling up (5)**.

12. My assignment is only for six months, so I'm not in the market for an unfurnished apartment. I need **the total package (15)** ASAP.

13. Bob Catelin is not one to blow his own horn. Case in point: he thinks Bobcat Beer is **small potatoes (12)**. I beg to differ. I think the sky is the limit.

14. Do you know what the **demographics (7)** are for the Upper East Side of Manhattan?

15. We need to face the music. **Word-of-mouth advertising (4)** has failed to increase our bottom-line. It's time to throw cold water on that idea.

## 8.C - The Story Continues - pg. 64

Steve:  Just between me and you, Mr. Catelin, Brad Clooney drinks Bobcat beer. And get this: he's got a bar in his Hollywood basement. This old English pub.

Bob:    Well, I'll be.

Steve:  Not only that, but he's got Bobcat Beer on tap. After a long day making movies, he goes down to his own private pub and pours himself a cold one.

Bob:    No fooling.

Steve:  Well? Should I give Mr. Clooney a call? Just say the word.

Bob:    I don't know. This is a tough call. I'm of two minds. Bobcat's always been a family business but at the end of the day, making money's the name of the game. Any businessman worth his salt knows that. And to do that, to make money, Bobcat's got to go national, no ifs, ands or buts. We've got to roll with the punches and run with the big boys.

Steve:  Look, why don't you sleep on it. Okay? I'll touch base with you tomorrow and we can go from there.

Bob:    Sounds like a plan. Now how about that beer?

## 8.D - Expansion - pg. 65

| | | | | | | | |
|---|---|---|---|---|---|---|---|
| 1. | H | 6. | S | 11. | J | 16. | T |
| 2. | Q | 7. | P | 12. | C | 17. | K |
| 3. | F | 8. | N | 13. | E | 18. | G |
| 4. | D | 9. | B | 14. | M | 19. | R |
| 5. | A | 10. | I | 15. | L | 20. | O |

## Review #2 ➔ Pg. 68

1.  In this dog-eat-dog world, if you want to **get your foot in the door** (19) you really have to **blow your own horn** (27), **no ifs, ands or buts** (5).

2.  We have to **face the music** (1), people. Sales are **a far cry from** (17) what they were last year. I think we need to give Brad Clooney his **walking papers** (15) and find a new **pitchman** (16).

3.  In this neck of the woods, office space will **set you back** (10) two grand a square foot. **Small potatoes** (9), really, compared to what's out there.

4.  Our **inventory** (2) is **piling up** (6). It's definitely going to put us **in the red** (11). What we need is a cash cow.

5.  You won't believe whom I sat beside on **the red eye** (12). Brad Clooney! The guy's a real **kick** (14). Rumor has it he's **raking it in** (25).

6.  Stop worrying about when you'll get your new laptop. You **have bigger fish to fry** (20), like researching the **demographics** (3) for Boston.

7.  **Let me lay it on the line** (21). It's **high time** (8) we started thinking outside the box. If not, we will continue to **spin our wheels** (24).

8.  **No one can hold a candle to** (22) Patricia. She is **the total package** (4).

9.  I want to **hang my hat** (26) here because it's **the only game in town** (23). By the way, I'm **a wiz at** (7) Photoshop and I make a great cup of **Joe** (13).

10. There is a big difference between **a freebie** (18) and a free ride.

## Lesson #9 ➔ *The Working Lunch* ➔ pg. 69

### 9.B - Practice - pg. 71

1.  We were about to seal the deal when the client **panned** (4) it completely.

2.  Rethinking that slogan is a waste of time. It's **water under the bridge** (10). Besides, we have bigger fish to fry.

3.  Revenue was up how much last quarter? **Run that by me again** (5).

4.  Sorry, but putting chocolate on a pizza is **a half-baked** idea (6).

5.  We just got our **marching orders** (8). It's time to roll up our sleeves and go to work.

6.  Bernie's been burning the midnight oil trying to make the client happy, yet he's just spinning his wheels. Believe me, he's **at the end of his rope** (11).

7.  Don't you just love **the twist** (12) at the end of that movie?

8. Amy, when you're finished running the numbers, send them out to each partner, okay? **You know the drill (15)**.

9. John was so hungry, he **scarfed down (14)** all the donuts.

10. Pete, are you on board? We've got to know. **The clock is running (9)**.

11. Charles is **under the gun (3)**. Everyone expects him to follow in his father's footsteps and take over the family business, but Charles is a far cry from his father. All Charles does is waffle.

12. No. Manhattan is not like Los Angeles. Los Angeles is **a whole different story (13)**.

13. Even though the problem is small potatoes, you still have to **work it through (2)**.

14. If you want to keep your job, you really have **to buckle down (1)** and hit one out of the park or else your head will be on the chopping block.

15. That restaurant looks expensive. It is full of **suits (7)**.

## 9.C - The Story Continues - pg. 72

Debra: Mom walks in all smiles and says, "Who wants dessert?" Everyone is surprised. Why? Because mom is holding an apple pie, a chocolate cake? No. It gets better. She's got another piping-hot Biagi pizza. The happy family cheers and digs in. They just can't get enough.

Rick: Pizza for dessert? I'll get back to you on that one.

Debra: It's not dessert. It's Biagi pizza. It's better than dessert. Hey, that can be our tagline: Biagi Pizza. Better than dessert.

Rick: Like I said, I'll get back to you.

Debra: I beg to differ. It touches all bases. Tradition. Family. Home. Beth? Correct me if I'm wrong, but that's what Biagi wants. Pure MOR Right?

Beth: You got it. Okay, people, so we have desert pizza and pizza for dessert. Let's flesh out a few more ideas before we nail this thing down.

## 9.D - Expansion - pg. 73

| | | | | | | | |
|---|---|---|---|---|---|---|---|
| 1. | K | 6. | R | 11. | D | 16. | I |
| 2. | N | 7. | L | 12. | F | 17. | E |
| 3. | A | 8. | P | 13. | G | 18. | J |
| 4. | M | 9. | S | 14. | T | 19. | O |
| 5. | B | 10. | C | 15. | H | 20. | Q |

## Lesson #10 → *The Power Lunch* → pg. 76

### 10.B - Practice - pg. 78

1. Many in America believe that the tax laws should be **overhauled** (3).

2. In this neck of the woods, if you want **to crack** (4) the coffee-shop market, you really have to think outside the box.

3. If you seal the deal, that means everyone is **on the same page** (14).

4. That hotel was great. They took care of everything, **from soup to nuts** (12).

5. What I admire about Joan is that she thinks outside the box and she takes no prisoners. She definitely **speaks my language** (8).

6. The bottom line is we need to start **pinching pennies** (9) or else we will end up in the red.

7. Joan will give this project **the green light** (10) only if we bring it in under budget.

8. Lidia jumped ship because her old company was **an old boys' club** (6) and she was just spinning her wheels.

9. I'm not going **to mince words** (2) We need to clean house and bring in new blood.

10. Joe thinks we should **branch out into** (1) the donut business. Personally, I think he's off his rocker. Dunkin Donuts will eat our lunch.

11. The slogan **per se** (7) is fine. You just have to flesh out some better ideas for the logo. And remember: the clock is running.

12. **Why mess with success** (5)? Because we've been resting on our laurels for too long. We have to put a fire under it and step up the plate.

13. Bob thought the board would pan his idea, but he **got buy-in** (13) instead. He is definitely a happy camper. Look at him. He looks like the cat that ate the canary.

14. Howard and Sally did what? Tell me. I'm **all ears** (15).

15. Maria **set** Joan **up with** (11) Abby Finestein, the best real estate agent in Manhattan.

### 10.C - The Story Continues - pg. 79

Joan:    I'm going to buy a place in the city. Nothing fancy, just a simple pied-à-terre.

Diana:    A simple pied-à-terre will cost you an arm and a leg—and then some.

Joan:     I know. That's why I'm going to sell some stock. Do you think I should <u>unload Apple</u> or just <u>sit on it</u>?

Diana:    I'd hold on to it. Apple's <u>product pipeline</u> is unsurpassed. I would, however, unload Microsoft. They've been <u>spinning their wheels</u> for years. Also, I've heard that the new Windows is <u>being trashed by beta testers</u>. That doesn't <u>augur well</u> for Mr. Gates.

Joan:     What about Amazon? Buy, sell, or hold?

Diana:    Buy it and hold it. Absolutely. Amazon is the biggest online retailer. Nobody even comes close. In ten years, you will double your money.

Joan:     What about commission? Is it still seven percent?

Diana:    Tell you what. Show me some logo designs and we'll talk about the commission. In the meantime, I've got <u>to skedaddle</u>. Call me. And say hello to Don for me. Let me know when you're going <u>to tie the knot</u>.

## 10.D - Expansion - pg. 80

| | | | | | | | |
|---|---|---|---|---|---|---|---|
| 1. | H | 6. | P | 11. | R | 16. | B |
| 2. | Q | 7. | J | 12. | N | 17. | K |
| 3. | I | 8. | D | 13. | T | 18. | G |
| 4. | A | 9. | S | 14. | C | 19. | E |
| 5. | L | 10. | F | 15. | O | 20. | M |

## Lesson #11 ➔ Mum's the Word ➔ pg. 83

### 11.B - Practice - pg. 85

1. Ali hopes his new invention will **fly (3)** in the American market.

2. **When push comes to shove (4)**, I will be there in a New York minute.

3. I hate **to sound like a broken record (6)**, but the sky is the limit.

4. Joan really **burst my bubble (11)** when she threw cold water on my idea.

5. If you don't **go over** your quarterly report **with a fine-tooth comb (14)**, the CFO will have kittens if she finds a mistake.

6. We thought our jobs were safe, but **at the eleventh hour (15)**, we all got pink slips. Suffice it to say, we are not happy campers.

7. Becoming president of the United States is a little **out of my league (10)**.

8. Remember what I said. If you don't **come through (7)**, you will have to face the music. You've been resting on your laurels for too long.

9. **Don't count your chickens before they are hatched (9)**. We still need to get buy-in from the CEO. If not, we'll just be spinning our wheels.

10. The first rule of business: **You don't get a second chance to make a first impression (13)**.

11. I love the new business plan. You really **nailed (5)** it, everything from soup to nuts.

12. I agree. Our corporate image is quite **stodgy (2)**, but why mess with success?

13. If you want to be a heavy hitter, you really need to **set your sights a little higher (12)** and start climbing the corporate ladder.

14. Mid-career movie stars often hit the reset button on their careers by doing **a make-over (1)** and taking jobs as product pitchmen.

15. After we pull out all the stops, the client is going to be **eating out of our hands (8)** and revenues will be through the roof.

## 11.C - The Story Continues - pg. 86

Judy: Should we take out a bank loan to cover short-term costs?
Joan: That won't be necessary. Our cash flow is fine. I just signed Hermes H2O.
Judy: Really? How did you pull that off?
Joan: Let's just say I have a knack for persuading people. I have a few more irons in the fire as well. One is with BMW.
Judy: Wow. You are on a roll. Have you announced it?
Joan: No. You can send out a memo about Hermes H2O, but Mum's the word on BMW. Like I said, let's not count our chickens before they're hatched.
Judy: Does the BMW account come with any, you know, freebies?
Joan: Like what? A few complimentary cars? I don't think so. What it does have is cachet. And that you can take to the bank.

## 11.D - Expansion - pg. 87

| | | | | | | | |
|---|---|---|---|---|---|---|---|
| 1. | T | 6. | J | 11. | R | 16. | E |
| 2. | M | 7. | O | 12. | C | 17. | F |
| 3. | N | 8. | B | 13. | D | 18. | G |
| 4. | A | 9. | K | 14. | P | 19. | L |
| 5. | Q | 10. | S | 15. | I | 20. | H |

# Lesson #12 → A Conflict of Interest → pg. 90

## 12.B - Practice - pg. 92

1. When push comes to shove, we will seal the deal. **Absolutely (2)**.

2. We've pulled out all the stops, but we are still **treading water (7)**.

3. Jill climbed the corporate ladder until she finally became the **general counsel (4)**.

4. Al asked if I would **give him my two cents (1)** on his latest invention. I did and told him it was half-baked and would never fly.

5. Sue just got the green light to go to Viet Nam to open a new branch office. That's a real **feather in her cap (10)**, especially in this old boys' club.

6. You just bought a new house and you need to buy a new car? What exactly are you **driving at (11)**? I take it you want a raise.

7. That guy is a bad penny. His hands **are** definitely not **clean (8)**.

8. Helena is in **a Catch-22 (15)**. If she works, she won't be able to finish school, but if she doesn't work, she won't be able to pay for school.

9. Dirk went over the contract with a fine-tooth comb, but I've already found three points that aren't boilerplate. Boy, did he **drop the ball (12)**.

10. The smell from that factory has really **tainted (9)** the air.

11. Mary just got a pink slip. She's not worried. She's **spinning it in a positive light (6)**. She thinks a change of companies will do her good.

12. It was high time Toni **made amends (13)** for losing the account.

13. I would love to work for Apple and Microsoft at the same time. Who wouldn't? But that, I'm afraid, would be **a conflict of interest (5)**.

14. Who is **giving the keynote (3)** at the conference? Rumor has it that Bill Gates is slated to speak. I would love to schmooze with him after.

15. Stop trying **to pull the wool over my eyes (14)**. I wasn't born yesterday.

## 12.C - The Story Continues - pg. 93

Judy: William and I had a falling out.
Beth: Over what?
Judy: Over where Debbie should go to university next year. William wants her to go to Princeton. She got accepted, but the tuition is outrageous.
Beth: Okay, so apply for a student loan.
Judy: Right. And when Debbie—who has never had a real job in a her life—graduates at 22, she'll be in debt to the tune of two-hundred thousand dollars. That is so criminal. The education system in this country makes me so mad. Kids are graduating with massive loans. How are they supposed to buy cars and houses, and start families when they're already saddled with so much debt? Once a university degree meant something, but now? In this economy? Ridiculous. And Washington is doing nothing about it. All they care about is getting re-elected by serving their corporate masters.

Beth:    Those corporate masters pay our salaries. But I do see what you're driving at. These days universities are simply <u>brands</u>, like a pair of jeans or sneakers. <u>That said</u>, <u>at the end of the day</u>, does Debbie want Princeton on her résumé or some <u>no-name college</u>?

<u>Judy</u>:    That's exactly what William said.

## 12.D - Expansion - pg. 94

| | | | | | | | |
|---|---|---|---|---|---|---|---|
| 1. | A | 6. | Q | 11. | D | 16. | T |
| 2. | K | 7. | B | 12. | E | 17. | I |
| 3. | N | 8. | C | 13. | F | 18. | J |
| 4. | O | 9. | R | 14. | G | 19. | S |
| 5. | P | 10. | M | 15. | H | 20. | L |

## Review #3 → Pg. 97

1. I hate to **sound like a broken record (19)**, but you need to **make to amends (27)** for **dropping the ball (1)** last week.

2. You really need to talk to the **general counsel (2)**. That is definitely a **conflict of interest (22)**. She will give you the bottom line.

3. I know what you are **driving at (18)**. Sorry, but I still think it is a **half-baked (10)** idea. It flies in the face of what **the suits (12)** want.

4. I'm **giving the keynote (9)** speech at the conference. It is really going to **fly (4)**. I have definitely **nailed (13)** it.

5. That guy is **a spin doctor (5)**. He's so glib. It's like he's always trying to **pull the wool over** our **eyes (25)**.

6. I hate to **burst your bubble (7)** but that suit is really **stodgy (20)**. What you need is **a make-over (17)**.

7. If you don't **set your sights a little higher (24)**, you will just **tread water (23)**.

8. Don't do a thing until you get the **green light (11)**. **You know the drill (3)**. And watch your budget. The company is really **pinching pennies (26)**.

9. Alice **panned (14)** my idea **at the eleventh hour (8)**. I really thought that I had her **eating out of my hand (6)**. I guess not.

10. The government is **under the gun (15)** to **overhaul (21)** the **old boys' club (16)** that is Wall Street.

## Lesson #13 → *Taking the Reins* → pg. 98

### 13.B - Practice - pg. 100

1. Please **jog my memory** (2). I can't remember who was on that ad hoc committee.

2. Bill has **a can-do attitude** (8). That's his M.O. As a result, he is always pulling out all the stops to climb the corporate ladder.

3. **Here's the deal** (10). At this company, you can't argue with the status quo. The boss is the boss, and she is as tough as nails.

4. Barry was so **swamped** (5) with work, he had to pull an all-nighter.

5. The company pulled the plug on its investment banking **division** (12) due to severe losses in the 2008 mortgage meltdown.

6. Jack is such a yes-man. He **strokes** the CEO's **ego** (9) ad nauseum.

7. Sorry, but you're backing up the wrong tree. I'd love to lend you a million dollars, but I'm really **strapped for** cash (6).

8. Before you buy that "pre-owned" BMW on eBay, you'd better take some time and **mull it over** (3). Remember what they say: caveat emptor.

9. We've got to hand it to Beth. When the new accountant suddenly jumped ship, Beth stepped up to the plate and **took the reins** (13).

10. I'd love to hob knob with Brad Clooney and his new wife, but I know I'd get **cold feet** (15). I'm not much of a schmoozer. It's just not my M.O.

11. We struck while the iron was hot and now we're raking money in **hand over fist** (7). At this rate, we will be in the black by next quarter.

12. Hank burned the midnight oil writing **copy** for the new KFC TV spot.

13. You can pick my brain all you want, but I'm telling you, it has completely **slipped my mind** (4).

14. Joe is so smooth. He can **charm the birds out of the trees** (14).

15. **Have** you **got what it takes** (11) to swim with sharks?

### 13.C - The Story Continues - pg. 101

Maria: Cold feet? No. Not at all. I'm definitely up for this. Totally.

Joan: Good. When you walk out of this office, I want you to hit the ground running. Here's a list of major corporations in Latin America.

Maria: Wow. So many.

Joan: That's just for starters. Call them up. Give them the elevator pitch. Tell them that Austen Advertising is poised to take them to the next level with the best creative team in the business and a financial staff second to none. Don't hang up until you <u>get your foot in the door</u>. Offer them lunch, dinner. Whatever it takes. You have to convince them that we are <u>the only game in town</u>.

Maria:     This is so unexpected. Really. I don't know how to thank you.

Joan:     Don't. You deserve it. You've always <u>gone the extra mile</u>. When it's <u>crunch time</u>, you've always <u>come through</u>. Anything else?

Maria:     Yes. Does this mean I get a raise?

Joan:     Bring me some good news and we'll talk. Oh, and you'll need to find and train a replacement—and get yourself an assistant.

## 13.D - Expansion - pg. 102

| | | | | | | | |
|---|---|---|---|---|---|---|---|
| 1. | H | 6. | R | 11. | K | 16. | J |
| 2. | A | 7. | Q | 12. | E | 17. | G |
| 3. | S | 8. | C | 13. | I | 18. | D |
| 4. | O | 9. | P | 14. | L | 19. | N |
| 5. | B | 10. | T | 15. | M | 20. | F |

## Lesson #14 → *The New Normal* → pg. 105

### 14.B - Practice - pg. 107

1. Working from home is quickly becoming **the new normal** (10).

2. Patti and Lily are going **to hook up** (5) over a working lunch to iron out the details in the letter-of-intent.

3. A bull market is **a seller's market** (13). Caveat emptor.

4. Joe, I know you always take no prisoners, but when you meet with the IRS next week, please **keep an open mind** (3).

5. I ran the numbers and, unfortunately, the PSF is **a bit too steep** (12). Is there any wiggle room?

6. Ann looks like the cat that ate the canary. It's **written all over her face** (11).

7. If you like that apartment, you'd better **grab it** (14). Seriously. In this neck of the woods, it will be gone in a New York minute.

8. Living in Manhattan is **to die for** (1). Absolutely. If that is your dream, then you'd better start climbing the corporate ladder.

9. During lunch, Elvia was able **to squeeze in a look at** (2) the new Audi over at the dealer's. She thinks it's a steal. I beg to differ.

10. When Swati saw the new iPad, it was **love at first sight** (4).

11. **When word gets out that (15)** we won't be getting bonuses this year, more than a few are going to hit the roof.

12. Car dealers always peddle the car with the most **bells and whistles (9)**.

13. Stop being so wishy-washy. If you don't step up to the plate and bid on that contract, you are going **to be kicking yourself for the rest of your life (6)**.

14. On TV, **state-of-the-art (8)** products, like the new Cadillac, are pitched using soft selling.

15. The best time **to list (7)** a house is in early spring.

## 14.C - The Story Continues - pg. 108

Joan: This place is much bigger than I need. Is the one in Tribeca still available?
Abby: Forget Tribeca. Trust me, in the long run, this place will give you more bang for your buck. Central Park West always sells even when the market tanks. It's money in the bank, believe me. And remember: a bird in hand is worth two in the bush.
Joan: It is rather nice. It should be for what they're asking.
Abby: Joanie, I hate to beat a dead horse, but it's high noon*, honey.
Joan: What about parking?
Abby: You get a space in the basement. Totally secure. (*Her cell phone rings, and rings*). The clock's running, Joanie. The wolves are at the door.
Joan: I'll take it.
Abby: Good girl. You won't regret it. This place is you all over.
Joan: Will they knock five percent off if I pay cash?
Abby: No harm in asking. What about your Greenwich place?
Joan: List it. It's time to move on.

## 14.D - Expansion - pg. 109

| | | | | | | | |
|---|---|---|---|---|---|---|---|
| 1. | K | 6. | S | 11. | Q | 16. | L |
| 2. | C | 7. | E | 12. | P | 17. | D |
| 3. | G | 8. | I | 13. | A | 18. | M |
| 4. | F | 9. | O | 14. | B | 19. | N |
| 5. | J | 10. | R | 15. | H | 20. | T |

# Lesson #15 ➜ *No Free Lunch* ➜ pg. 112

## 15.B - Practice - pg. 114

1. If I were you, I'd fix up your house, then list it. Right now, it's not **ready for prime time (1)**.

2. Tom might be able to charm the birds out of the trees, but in his monthly reports, he never **dots his i's or crosses his t's (2)**.

3. Joan does not want back-of-the-envelope calculations. She is **a stickler for detail (3)**. Please give her the final numbers.

4. Another upgrade? That's the second one this year. Microsoft is **nothing if not predictable (5)**.

5. The Waldorf Astoria **caters to (6)** the noveau riche and to old money.

6. **Road warriors (7)** love freebies because they are usually on tight budgets.

7. Retailers who target **niche markets (8)** are closed on Black Friday.

8. I'm **calling the shots (11)** around here. It's either my way or the highway.

9. At the eleventh hour, the board **ponied up (13)** the cash needed to complete the project on time.

10. I'd love to give you a corner office, but **my hands are tied (10)**.

11. Once a year, the world's **movers and shakers (9)** meet in Davos, Switzerland to discus world problems and to schmooze.

12. This laptop is **the bane of my existence (4)**. It is always crashing. I wish Dell would step up to the plate and replace it.

13. It's high time we gave Maria a raise. Since she came on board, she's been doing **a bang-up job (15)**. She has a real can-do attitude.

14. Sorry, but we can't make lemonade out of lemons on **a shoe-string budget (12)**.

15. In this firm, there are **no free lunches (14)**. At the end of the day, bill the client for everything—pencils, stamps, coffee—the works.

## 15.C – The Story Continues – pg. 115

(*Later Rick and Beth eat pizza at a pizza joint.*)

Rick: When I grabbed a coffee at Mickey-D's this morning, I noticed that they've got oatmeal and blueberries on the menu.

Beth: Healthy fast-food is the new normal. Fast-food chains are waking up to the fact that their customers are becoming more health conscious. Did you know that eight million Americans have diabetes and that 79 million have prediabetes?

Rick: Amazing.

Beth: High-fructose corn syrup is the culprit. It's in everything. I don't touch the stuff. I read every label before I buy.

Rick: You on a diet?

Beth: Isn't everyone? So what was the coffee like?

Rick:    At Mickey D's? Great. It wasn't <u>run-of-the-mill</u> at all. It was a medium roast. For a buck, you can get a small, medium or large. Your choice for a buck! I don't know how Starbucks competes. They're <u>pricing themselves out of the market</u>. What?

Beth:    Are you going to eat that last slice?

Rick:    <u>Knock yourself out.</u>

## 15.D - Expansion - pg. 116

| | | | | | | | |
|---|---|---|---|---|---|---|---|
| 1. | Q | 6. | B | 11. | T | 16. | J |
| 2. | G | 7. | O | 12. | D | 17. | P |
| 3. | H | 8. | R | 13. | E | 18. | K |
| 4. | M | 9. | N | 14. | F | 19. | L |
| 5. | A | 10. | C | 15. | I | 20. | S |

## Lesson #16 ➜ *Pushing My Buttons* ➜ pg. 119

## 16.B - Practice - pg. 121

1. Hector is a wiz at **tracing (8)** computer problems.

2. In Manhattan, trying to beat the traffic is **for the birds (3)**.

3. No raise? Again? That's **the last straw (4)**. Tomorrow, I intend to jump ship. This accounting firm is not the only game in town.

4. Let me lay it on the line. This company will never be **a fast-follower (10)**. We'll always make state-of-the-art products for an upscale, niche market.

5. No, I did not **touch base with (15)** that company. Why not? Because they're small potatoes. We have much bigger fish to fry.

6. Joe had **a melt down (2)** when Joan told him that his idea was half-baked. No surprise there. Joe is nothing if not predictable.

7. What's good for my ego? When I **deliver (12)**.

8. Your report is great. A real bang-up job. You don't have to change a thing. **Leave well enough alone (5)** until you get more feedback.

9. People who are anal often end up **shooting themselves in the foot (6)** because they can never leave well enough alone.

10. If you want to take a shot at swimming with the sharks, you'd better leave the **TLC (14)** at home. Trust me, heavy hitters take no prisoners.

11. I'm glad Diana is well and **back in business (13)**. She has always been a tower of strength.

12. Tailgaters really **push my buttons (1)**.

13. Ever since Apple introduced the iPad, the market has been flooded with **me-too products (11)**, many of which are sold at big-box stores.

14. Some say, "Upgrade." I say, "**If it ain't broke, don't fix it (7)**."

15. This printer is so slow. I swear, the thing **has a mind of its own (9)**.

## 16.C - The Story Continues - pg. 122

Joan:     Yes. Call the Apple <u>rep</u>. But don't sign anything before you bring me the numbers. I don't want <u>to be taken to the cleaners</u>, all right?

Hector:     Understand. *(exiting)* Let me know if you have any more <u>hiccups</u>.

Joan:     You'll be the first to know, believe me.

Maria:     Joan? Aren't you lunching tomorrow with Sylvia Smith, Microsoft's V.P. of marketing?

Joan:     I am. So?

Maria:     So why don't you tell her enough with the upgrades? Serious. Somebody should do <u>a productivity study</u> and figure out how many working-hours employees lose every year wasting time trying to relearn software updates or waiting for updates to install.

Joan:     Then what?

Maria:     Then all those companies that have lost time should send the bill to Microsoft and <u>sue</u> for compensation.

## 16.D - Expansion - pg. 123

| | | | | | | | |
|---|---|---|---|---|---|---|---|
| 1. | O | 6. | A | 11. | C | 16. | N |
| 2. | I | 7. | M | 12. | Q | 17. | J |
| 3. | T | 8. | P | 13. | G | 18. | F |
| 4. | L | 9. | R | 14. | D | 19. | K |
| 5. | S | 10. | B | 15. | E | 20. | H |

## Review #4 → Pg. 126

1. Even though the company is **strapped for cash (19)**, everyone still has a **can-do attitude (20)** and is ready to **lend a hand (1)** where needed.

2. Ann is very **buttoned-down (2)**. In this office, she **calls the shots (14)** and is a **stickler for details (5)**.

3. If you're living on a **shoe-string budget (13)**, here's the deal. Avoid retailers that **cater to (18)** the **nouveau riche (22)**.

4. That **penthouse (10)** is **to die for (9)**. Everything is **state-of-the art (26)**. Best of all, it's a **buyer's market (3)**.

5.  There is definitely a **method to** Chuck's **madness** (23). There must be. He's making money **hand-over fist** (17).

6.  We're going to win **hands down** (4) because we **hold all the cards** (8).

7.  I can't believe it. Manuel is a **rainmaker** (11), but he asked me to **pony up** (16) for lunch. Doesn't that guy know there are **no free lunches** (25)?

8.  I asked Wioleta to **take the reins** (21) and **rein in** (7) costs. I also told her to not **cut corners** (6) even if production is **down to the wire** (24).

9.  I **touched base with** (15) the client and gave her the pitch. She said she'd **mull it over** (12) and get back to me ASAP.

10. Staying on a diet is **the bane of my existence** (27).

## Lesson #17 ➜ *Legal Advice* ➜ pg. 127

### 17.B - Practice - pg. 129

1.  That idea is a long shot. If it doesn't fly, I will **lose my shirt** (12).

2.  **Figuratively speaking** (13), if the shoe fits, wear it.

3.  When you finally decide **to set up shop** (3), remember: location, location, location.

4.  Carla is a great boss. I'm always **bending her ear** (1) about something.

5.  Many law firms are **limited partnerships** (8).

6.  Anthony has always been a rainmaker, but lately his pitches have failed **to take off** (2). He seems to be spinning his wheels.

7.  Revenues are up. So is productivity. Employee morale is also hitting new highs. The company is definitely **firing on all cylinders** (4).

8.  How does taking a trip to Hawaii **fit in** (5) to your business plan? Run that by me again. I want to make sure we're on the same page.

9.  **In light of** (7) the fact that their last offer was a deal breaker, I'm of a mind to pull the plug and go bang the drum elsewhere.

10. The bottom line is we need to build environmentally friendly oil rigs. If we don't, we are going **to be liable** (15) for every drop of oil we spill.

11. Mike, you will go and talk to the client. The client will, **in turn** (14), report back to Sally as to their final decision.

12. Sure, you got axed, but **the upside is** (12) you are now free to start your own business, you know, the one you've always talked about.

13. I've told Barney he should really incorporate to protect his personal assets, but he says **a sole proprietorship (6)** is all he really needs.

14. Many point to the Dutch East India Company as being the world's first **corporation (9)**.

15. **In a nutshell (10)**, I think we have been fast-followers far too long. It is time to think outside the box and hit one out of the park.

## 17.C - The Story Continues - pg. 130

Don:   With a corporation, you'd have <u>to go public</u>. You'd sell <u>shares</u> and basically <u>be beholden to your shareholders</u>. You'd have to get a bank <u>to underwrite your IPO</u>, hold annual <u>shareholder meetings</u>, and perform <u>myriad</u> other corporation functions all <u>in the public eye</u>. However, as a sole proprietor, you'd remain private, as you would with a limited partnership.

Joan:   So what do you recommend?

Don:   I recommend dinner and a Yankee's game. Between innings, I can elaborate on the finer points of each business <u>entity</u>. Shall I <u>pencil you in for Saturday night</u>?

Joan:   You <u>drive a hard bargain</u>, counselor.

Don:   I hate to rush you, but I have the Canadian ambassador <u>parked on the other line</u>.

Joan:   What's he want?

Don:   Sorry, <u>attorney-client privilege</u>. So, what's it going to be?

Joan:   Well, since you did give me free legal advice, I will attend your <u>soirée</u> tonight. It's at the Waldorf, right?

Don:   Yes. The party starts at 8:00. Do you need <u>a lift</u>?

Joan:   I'm fine, thanks. I'll see you there.

## 17.D - Expansion - pg. 131

| | | | |
|---|---|---|---|
| 1. T | 6. A | 11. R | 16. H |
| 2. N | 7. Q | 12. E | 17. I |
| 3. M | 8. B | 13. S | 18. J |
| 4. O | 9. C | 14. F | 19. K |
| 5. P | 10. D | 15. G | 20. L |

# Lesson #18 ➜ *From the Ground Up* ➜ pg. 134

## 18.B - Practice - pg. 136

1. The scuttlebutt is Ray, who is always blowing his horn, quickly climbed the corporate ladder by **riding on** his uncle Phil's **coattails (12)**.

2. You took the words right out of my mouth. Patti is so **down-to-earth (14)**.

3.  Let me **cut to the chase** (4). You don't get a second chance to make a first impression.

4.  Some of my coworkers are quite happy **pushing paper** (6) all day. Not me. One of these days I'm going to be an A-player calling the shots.

5.  This job **entails** (5) taking the red-eye to Boston once a week. Why so much travel? Because spending face-time with clients is important.

6.  Dave's work hasn't **been up to scratch** (10) lately. He's not dotting his i's or crossing his t's. Personally, I think he's about to jump ship.

7.  My boss is such **a slave driver** (9). Every morning she gives me my marching orders and says, "You know the drill. Don't drop the ball."

8.  Al's skill set got his foot in the door. Now he's waiting for **a call back** (3).

9.  We need to face the music and bring in new blood **from the ground up** (15).

10. It's time to roll up our sleeves and **put our noses to the grindstone** (13).

11. Mary, I'm swamped. Can you **go** to that conference **in my stead** (8)?

12. Tom **jumped all over** (11) Cindy when she said that this company was nothing more than a stodgy old boys' club in need of an overhaul.

13. Here's the deal. You can't work legally in the U.S. without **a green card** (1).

14. Before you sign up for the Diversity Immigrant Visa **lottery** (2), make sure your hands are clean. If you win a green card, before you get it, U.S. immigration will go over your personal history with a fine-tooth comb.

15. You really need to buckle down and learn how **to navigate** the new computer **system** (7). We have a lot riding on it.

## 18.C - The Story Continues - pg. 137

Maria:  In a year or two, if all goes as planned, you'll be responsible for your own accounts. However, you are not finished school yet. You have one more year. So, what do you think? Would you like to sleep on it?

Talita:  Are you kidding? I'm psyched. Totally. I accept. You know what they say: you snooze, you lose.

Maria:  In that case, Ms. Alves, congratulations. Welcome to Austen Advertising. Come by tomorrow morning and we can get the ball rolling.

Talita:  Great. By the way, what are the benefits?

Maria:  You get complete dental and medical. Each has a two-hundred-and-fifty-dollar deductible. You can also enroll in a 401K.

Talita:  Sweet. One more thing. Where's my office?

Maria:  Sorry. No office. Just a cubicle. Is that a problem?

Talita:  No. I'm just happy I've got a job. Thanks again. See you tomorrow.

Maria:  Eight o'clock on the dot.

Talita:  I'll be here. Bye.

## 18.D - Expansion - pg. 138

| | | | | | | | |
|---|---|---|---|---|---|---|---|
| 1. | E | 6. | O | 11. | G | 16. | J |
| 2. | N | 7. | B | 12. | R | 17. | S |
| 3. | L | 8. | P | 13. | H | 18. | T |
| 4. | A | 9. | F | 14. | M | 19. | C |
| 5. | K | 10. | Q | 15. | I | 20. | D |

## Lesson #19 ➜ *Crossing the Rubicon* ➜ pg. 141

### 19.B - Practice - pg. 143

1. Uri in marketing deserves a big **pat on the back (10)** for finally getting the show on the road.

2. Aya is just **itching to (9)** put the pedal to the metal and seal the deal.

3. Suffice it to say, a laptop is not **eco-friendly (4)**. Why not? Let's cut to the chase. A laptop, from making to recycling, produces 350 kg of C02, which is comparable to 240 liters of orange juice.

4. We haven't **cut a deal (5)** with Apple per se. As I said, we are still just talking. Hopefully, an LOI is right around the corner.

5. Be prepared for **sticker shock (1)** when you look for houses in this neck of the woods. It is definitely upscale.

6. Ahmad sure can **talk the talk**, but when push comes to shove, he sure can't **walk the walk (11)**.

7. Do not hire that man. He's **sending the wrong vibe (3)**. It's obvious that he's trying to pull the wool over our eyes.

8. No more coffee or tea? This company is really **feeling the pinch (12)**.

9. Even though Alok is a slave driver, I always manage to **weather the storm (13)**, like water off a duck's back.

10. When I arrived in Tokyo for the first time, I looked around and said, "**Toto, I have a feeling we're not in Kansas anymore (2)**."

11. You got a twenty-percent raise? How did you **swing (15)** that?

12. You have a nice house, but your roof is not up to scratch. Here's the deal. I will buy your house if you **throw in (6)** a new roof.

13. If you are in a Catch-22, no matter which way you choose, you will end up **crossing the Rubicon (7)**.

14. Francesco **looks as nervous as a cat in a room full of rocking chairs (8)**. If he doesn't get a call back, he's going to be pounding the pavement again.

15. Markuss would love **to hook (14)** a green card. His dream is to set up shop in America. He hates his current job. Pushing paper all day for a big corporation is not his cup of tea.

## 19.C - The Story Continues - pg. 144

Joan:   How did I <u>hook Ms. Jane Frost</u>? Simple. I told her there's no <u>glass ceiling</u> at Austen Advertising. Also, she's agreed <u>to head up our London office</u>. She's from London, so she <u>jumped at the chance</u>.
Maria:  I've heard she can be <u>a handful</u>.
Joan:   It <u>comes with the territory</u>. You want the best? You get the best, and everything else that comes with it. But think about it: when the deal is <u>on the line</u>, when you are fighting for every <u>slice of the pie</u>, who do you want <u>in your corner</u>? A poodle or <u>a shark</u>?
Maria:  Have you announced it?
Joan:   No. I'll send out a memo after we move in. But for now, <u>Mum's the word</u> on Ms. Frost. Have you seen your new office? Come. Have a look. Well? What do you think?
Maria:  A corner office? Oh, my god!

## 19.D - Expansion - pg. 145

| | | | | | | | |
|---|---|---|---|---|---|---|---|
| 1. | R | 6. | I | 11. | N | 16. | C |
| 2. | A | 7. | J | 12. | O | 17. | S |
| 3. | Q | 8. | T | 13. | G | 18. | D |
| 4. | H | 9. | K | 14. | P | 19. | E |
| 5. | L | 10. | M | 15. | B | 20. | F |

## Lesson #20 ➔ All's Well that Ends Well ➔ pg. 148

## 20.B - Practice - pg. 150

1. When Ali stepped off the plane at JFK for the first time, he had no time **to feel like a fish out of water (1)**. He had to hit the ground running and meet a client.

2. Yasemin is **rolling in it (8)**. Why? Because she always puts her nose to the grindstone and is never afraid to go out on a limb and up the ante.

3. I've heard through **the grapevine (12)** that Adam would throw his own grandmother under the bus to seal that deal.

4. Alok is definitely **sitting pretty (6)**. It's a seller's market and his house has curb appeal and, best of all, location, location, location.

5. Lars loves **to work/working a room (4)**. He says it's good for his ego.

6. Good morning, everybody. This **run-down (5)** on the new database will be brief. Suffice it to say, I'm still learning how to navigate it.

7. Have you seen the attendee list? It's **a who's who (2)** of the film industry. Bear in mind, though, the conference fee is through the roof.

8. When Onur learned that his company had been cutting corners for years, he wanted **to crawl inside a hole and die (3)**.

9. Look at him. Asleep at the wheel again. **Earth to (7)** Richard. Hel-lo? We are leaving. Hel-lo?

10. Pitching over the phone is a tough putt, I know. The trick is to state the bottom line from the get-go and always **keep your eye on the prize (13)**.

11. Mark was always telling me **to keep it on the up and up (14)** when he was the one caught red-handed stealing pens from the store room.

12. There's a big difference between **powdering one's nose (9)** and taking a powder. The latter means "chilling" while the former means freshening up.

13. Excuse me? Can you tell me where **the little girl's/boy's room (10)** is?

14. **The cat is out of the bag (15)**. Yes, I did indeed win a green card.

15. Writing ESL text books is his **bread-and-butter (11)**. One day, he will publish a novel, but until then he will continue to write for his niche market.

## 20.C - The Story Continues - pg. 151

*(Don crosses the lobby of the Waldorf and approaches Joan.)*

Joan:    So is it official? Is your name on the shingle?
Don:     It is. They've also given me two weeks off. How does Tahiti sound?
Joan:    Tahiti sounds divine, but...
Don:     Hawaii? I could teach you how to surf.
Joan:    You know I'm transitioning into a new space.
Don:     Pizza and a movie?
Joan:    Stop.
Don:     So what should I do?
Joan:    Take a rain check?
Don:     The story of my life. C'mon. They're serving dinner. I ordered you vegan.
Joan:    Great. I'm starved.
Don:     You know what?
Joan:    What?
Don:     I think this is the beginning of a beautiful friendship.*

*\* See Movie-TV quotes on pg. 214*

*(They enter the dining room, arm in arm.)*

## 20.D - Expansion - pg. 152

| | | | | | | | |
|---|---|---|---|---|---|---|---|
| 1. | E | 6. | C | 11. | Q | 16. | O |
| 2. | B | 7. | S | 12. | G | 17. | N |
| 3. | M | 8. | D | 13. | I | 18. | K |
| 4. | F | 9. | H | 14. | P | 19. | L |
| 5. | T | 10. | R | 15. | J | 20. | A |

## Review #5 → Pg. 155

1. I think we should give Ian **a call back** (6). He **fits the bill** (10) and seems like a **down-to-earth** (1) guy.

2. When there is a lot of **red tape** (20), it is hard to **beat the system** (25). In that case, you just have to **play by the book** (9).

3. Management has **zero tolerance for** (8) **boondoggles** (11). When you attend that conference in Vegas, remember to **keep it on the up-and-up** (27) or else you will get your walking papers.

4. I really need to **scale back** my **hours** (26) and reassess my **work-life balance** (16) **from the ground up** (24).

5. Mick deserves **a pat on the back** (2) for **cutting a deal with** (22) Coca Cola. Mick is a real **up-and-comer** (21). Keep your eye on him.

6. The company intends to **make a splash** (17) by **setting up shop** (13) in every major city in the U.S. It is a **calculated risk** (3), but the **prospects** (19) look good.

7. You have to have **a thick skin** (4) working with Mike. He is such a **taskmaster** (14). You really have to **earn your stripes** (23).

8. Margaret is just **itching to** (12) pitch **eco-friendly** (7) products.

9. This market is not an **even playing field** (5). The government keeps **moving the goal posts** (15) for the benefit of domestic producers.

10. In business, the **margin of error** (18) is very small, indeed.

# The ICAO Spelling Alphabet

Years ago, English became the official language of commercial flying. However, English-speaking pilots were not enough. Airline pilots had to pronounce the same way when speaking English. By doing so, flight instructions would be clearer and flying safer. The ICAO (International Civil Aviation Organization) did all that by implementing the ICAO Spelling Alphabet (see chart below). This spelling alphabet is an essential communication tool not only for flying but for business as well. This is how I spell my name <u>Bruce</u> using this system.

"Bruce. B <u>for</u> Bravo. R <u>for</u> Romeo. U <u>for</u> uniform. C <u>for</u> Charlie. E <u>for</u> echo."

Note how I always put <u>for</u> between the letter and the code word. Look at the next example. Note how I just say the code words.

"Bruce. Bravo. Romeo. Uniform. Charlie. Echo."

**<u>Task</u>** ➔ Learn how to spell your full name using this system. Practice until you can spell your name automatically. Do the same with your company name, school name, your email address, work address—everything.

| A | for | alpha (al-fah) |
|---|-----|----------------|
| B | for | bravo (brah-voh) |
| C | for | Charlie (Char-lee) |
| D | for | delta (dell-tah) |
| E | for | echo (eck-oh) |
| F | for | foxtrot (foks-trot) |
| G | for | golf (golf) |
| H | for | hotel (hoh-tel) |
| I | for | India (In-dee-ah) |
| J | for | Juliet (Jew-lee-ett) |
| K | for | kilo (kee-loh) |
| L | for | Lima (Lee-mah) |
| M | for | Mike (Mike) |
| N | for | November (No-vem-ber) |
| O | for | Oscar (Oss-car) |
| P | for | papa (pah-pah) |
| Q | for | Quebec (Ka-bec) |
| R | for | Romeo (Row-may-oh) |
| S | for | sierra (see-air-rah) |
| T | for | tango (tang- go) |
| U | for | uniform (you-nee-form) |
| V | for | Victor (Vik-ter) |
| W | for | whiskey (wiss-key) |
| X | for | x-ray (ecks-ray) |
| Y | for | yankee (yang-key) |
| Z | for | Zulu (Zoo-loo) |

# Idiom and Word List

## A

A-player (an)
 - *a heavy hitter; a power player*
abandon ship (to)
 - *to give up; to throw in the towel*
absolutely
 - *yes/of course/certainly/by all means*
ad hoc (Latin)
 - *temporarily for a specific purpose*
ad nauseum (Latin)
 - *to repeat endlessly*
after the bell
 - *after the New York Stock Exchange (NYSE) closes at 4:00 pm*
ageism
 - *age discrimination*
all bright-eyed and bushy-tailed (to be)
 - *to be young and enthusiastic*
all ears (to be)
 - *to be listening closely*
all set (to be)
 - *to be ready*
all the rage (to be)
 - *to be fashionable/trendy/popular*
alpha
 - *"A" type; A-player; the strongest*
alpha male (an)
 - *top dog; dominant player*
ambush marketing
 - *advertising free in a competitor's paid-for market*
ameliorate (to)
 - *to make better; to improve*
amendment
 - *an adjustment/correction*
anal (to be)
 - *to be a stickler for detail*
and get this...
 - *and listen to this...*
and then some
 - *and more*

annoy (to)
 - *to bother/irritate*
arrive on the button (to)
 - *to show up at exactly the right time*
artery (an)
 - *a connecting road/highway*
ASAP
 - *as soon as possible*
as easy as pie (to be)
 - *to be no problem; a piece of cake*
as tough as nails (to be)
 - *to be strong/determined*
asleep at the wheel (to be)
 - *to be paying no attention; negligent*
asset (an)
 - *a thing of value that creates income*
at a crossroads (to be)
 - *to be facing a difficult choice*
at a premium (to be)
 - *to be expensive and in short supply*
at the eleventh hour
 - *at the last minute/second*
at the end of one's rope (to be)
 - *to have run out of patience/options*
at the end of the day...
 - *in the final analysis...; when all is said and done...*
at the top of one's game (to be)
 - *to be performing one's best*
attorney-client privilege
 - *the right of the attorney and client to keep all issues raised between them private; doctor-patient privilege*
augur well (for)(to)
 - *to look good (for)*
axiom (an)
 - *a statement accepted as true*

## B

back in business (to be)
 - *to be fixed; to be ready once again*
back-of-the-envelope calculations
 - *a rough estimate on paper*

backseat driver (a)
- *someone always telling you what to do without invitation or request*

bad blood
- *bad relations*

bad penny (a)
- *a person with a bad reputation*

bagged (to be)
- *to be exhausted; very tired*

bail out of (to)
- *to exit from*

bailout (to)
- *to rescue with financial help*

bane of one's existence (the)
- *something that causes one constant problems/pressure/headaches*

bang-on (to be)
- *to be perfect/exact*

bang the drum (to)
- *to support/promote enthusiastically*

bang-up job (a)
- *a job well done*

bark up the wrong tree (to)
- *to ask the wrong person; to move in the wrong direction*

bash (a)
- *a party*

be all ears (to be)
- *to be listening closely*

bear fruit (to)
- *to show positive results*

bear in mind (to)
- *to remember/consider*

bear market (a)
- *the prolonged selling/holding of securities and commodities; a sign of a weak economy*

beat a dead horse (to)
- *to continue to argue when debate is over*

beat around the bush (to)
- *to go around in circles; to miss the point*

beat the system (to)
- *to gain by breaking or bending the rules*

beat the traffic (to)
- *to avoid rush-hour by leaving early*

before the bell
- *before the New York Stock Exchange (NYSE) opens at 9:30 a.m.*

beg to differ (to)
- *to disagree respectfully*

beholden to someone (to be)
- *to be in a position of owing something to someone*

bells and whistles
- *extra features*

bend one's ear (to)
- *to ask for advice*

bend over backwards (to)
- *to try hard to please; to go the extra mile*

best shot
- *best try/attempt*

beta testers
- *those who test new software prior to commercial release*

bid (to)
- *to offer a price*

big-box store (a)
- *large retail store, i.e., Wal-Mart*

big guns (the)
- *heavy hitters; A-players; big dogs*

bird in hand is worth two in the bush (a)
- *the actual possession of one object is more valuable than two objects that are only imagined*

bit (too) steep (to be a)
- *to be (too) expensive*

bite the bullet (to)
- *to make a difficult decision*

blabbermouth (a)
- *one who talks too much; a rumormonger*

black eye (a)
- *a mark of shame/failure*

Black Friday
- *Thanksgiving Friday; a day of sales in the U.S.; the start of the Christmas shopping season*

Black Tuesday
- *October 29, 1929; the stock market crashed signaling the start of the Great Depression*

blockbuster (a)
- *a big financial success*

blow one's (own) horn (to)
- *to brag/boast; to self promote*
blow something (to)
- *to make a big mistake; to screw up*
blow something out of proportion (to)
- *to make a mountain out of a molehill*
blowback
- *an unexpected/unwanted effect*
blue collar
- *labor; blue work shirt no tie*
boilerplate (to be)
- *standard legal language/legalese*
bombshell (a)
- *a big and unexpected surprise*
bonus (a)
- *incentive; a reward for performing well*
boondoggle (a)
- *a waste of time and money*
bottleneck (a)
- *a narrow point in a road slowing traffic*
bottom line (the)
- *the message; the conclusion*
bottom out (to)
- *to hit the bottom*
braggart (a)
- *one who always blows his/her horn*
brainstorm (to)
- *to problem solve in a group or individually through the free-association of ideas*
branch (office)
- *an office separate from the main office*
branch out into something (to)
- *to expand into; to diversify*
brand (a)
- *a class of goods identified by a product name or symbol, i.e. Nike*
bread-and-butter (to be one's)
- *one's main source of income*
bread-winner (the)
- *one who brings money home*
brewski (a)
- *a beer*
brewskies
- *plural of beer*

brick-and-mortar (a)
- *a traditional retail store*
bridge the gap (to)
- *to make a connection between opposites*
bring something in under budget (to)
- *to complete a project, etc., below the budgeted cost*
brought up to speed on something (to be)
- *to be updated on the latest events*
brush up on something (to)
- *to review*
buckle down (to)
- *to get serious and work*
bull market (a)
- *the high-volume trading of securities and commodities with prices rising; a sign of a strong economy*
bump in the road (a)
- *a problem*
burden (a)
- *a heavy load/responsibility*
burned (to be)
- *to be ripped off/cheated*
burn a hole in one's pocket (to)
- *money you want to spend*
burn daylight (to)
- *to waste time*
burn one's bridges (to)
- *to make a decision that will have negative consequences resulting in a loss of personal/business connections*
burn the candle at both ends (to)
- *to burn the midnight oil; to work 24/7*
burn the midnight oil (to)
- *to work late often to meet a deadline; to burn the candle at both ends*
burning question (the)
- *the $64,000.00 question*
burst at the seams (to)
- *to break open and overflow*
burst one's bubble (to)
- *to wake one up to reality*
business entity (a)
- *a business type*

business plan (a)
- *a formal statement describing a company's goals and how they will attain them*

button up (to)
- *to keep silent*

buttoned down (to be)
- *to be conservative/traditional*

buy, sell, or hold (to)
- *the three options one has when buying and selling stock*

buyer's market (a)
- *a market with high inventory resulting in competitive prices*

buzz (the)
- *word-of-mouth advertising; the latest news; the rumor*

by all means
- *yes/of course/certainly*

# C

cachet
- *prestige; unique value*

call back (a)
- *a phone call inviting a prospective candidate to return for an interview*

call the shots (to)
- *to give orders*

can (to)
- *to fire/axe*

canary in the coal mine (the)
- *a warning sign*

can-do attitude (a)
- *the belief that nothing is impossible*

capitulate (to)
- *to surrender/give up; to throw in the towel; to raise the white flag*

case in point
- *for example...*

cash cow (a)
- *a reliable source of income from an established brand/product, etc.*

cash flow
- *money entering and leaving*

cat is out of the bag (the)
- *the secret is out*

catch someone in the act (to)
- *to catch someone red-headed*

catch someone red-handed (to)
- *to catch a person stealing*

Catch-22 (a)
- *to be faced with two bad choices; a no-win situation*

cater (to)
- *to serve/provide what is needed*

caveat emptor (Latin)
- *Let the buyer beware.*

charm the birds out of the trees (to)
- *to persuade anyone of anything*

chicken feed (to be)
- *a very small amount of money; chump change*

chug along (to)
- *to move at a constant speed*

chump change
- *an insignificant amount of money*

circle back to something (to)
- *to return to a topic at a later time/date*

clean (to be)
- *to be free of corruption/blame*

clean house (to)
- *to fire/lay off employees*

clean up (to)
- *to win decisively*

climb the corporate ladder (to)
- *to advance in a company through promotions*

clock is running (the)
- *the deadline is approaching; time is running out*

closer (a)
- *one who can persuade another to sign a contract/seal a deal, etc.*

cold call (to)
- *to sell/pitch something by phone*

cold one (a)
- *a cold beer*

come on the market (to)
- *to be made available for purchase*

come through (to)
- *to perform as expected; to arrive*

come with the territory (to)
- *to include the good and the bad*

commission
- *the percentage an agent/broker etc., makes from a sale*

commodity (a)
- *a raw product sold in bulk; oil, gold, bauxite, etc.*

complement (a)
- *a product of less value that sells with a main product, i.e., buns are the complement of hot dogs*

compliant (to be)
- *to follow the rules/laws; to conform*

complimentary
- *free*

condo (a)
- *building in which individual units are privately owned*

conflict of interest (a)
- *representing two opposing parties with different/conflicting interests*

consumer traffic
- *the number of people moving through a retail area in a business day*

conundrum (a)
- *a mystery/problem/puzzle*

co-op (a)
- *residential building owned and managed by the residents*

copy
- *script; the written part of an ad*

core competency
- *area of expertise; main skills*

corner office (a)
- *a symbol of success/rank*

corner the market (to)
- *to control all parts of a market*

corporate masters
- *corporations who support politicians with large donations in return for political influence*

corporation (a)
- *a business that is a legal entity separate from its owners*

Correct me if I'm wrong, but...
- *Please confirm that what I am saying is accurate/right, etc.*

cost an arm and a leg (to)
- *to be extremely expensive*

counselor (a)
- *a lawyer/attorney; legal counsel*

count one's chickens before they are hatched (to not)
- *to warn against assuming you have a gain before it is realized*

cover something (to)
- *to pay for something*

cozy-little
- *warm and small; nice and comfortable; just right*

crack something (to)
- *to enter a market, etc.*

crash (to)
- *to go down; to fail dramatically*

crash course (a)
- *an intensive course in which much is learned in little or no time*

crawl inside a hole and die (to)
- *to hide due to embarrassment*

critical mass
- *the minimum amount to start/maintain a business/process*

cross that bridge when one comes to it (to)
- *to deal with a problem/issue at the time, not before*

cross the line (to)
- *to cross the point of no return*

cross the Rubicon (to)
- *to cross the point of no return; historically the start of the Great Roman Civil War when Caesar crossed the Rubicon River.*

crunch the numbers (to)
- *to do financial calculations; to run the numbers*

crunch time
- *the time just before a deadline when the pressure to perform is the greatest*

cubicle (a)
- *a small square office space with no door, low walls, and carpeted walls*

culprit (the)
- *the object of blame; the bad guy*

cut a deal with someone (to)
- *to seal the deal*

cut-and-dry (to be)
- *to be straightforward/clear*

cut corners (to)
- *to reduce costs by using inferior material/bypassing accepted practices*

cut off one's nose to spite one's face (to)
- *to fail to see the negative consequences of one's actions*

cut out to be something/someone (to be)
- *to feel born to do; to be destined*

cut to the chase (to)
- *to state the bottom line*

cut your own throat (to)
- *to shoot yourself in the foot*

cute as a button (to be)
- *to be cute/adorable*

# D

daycation (a)
- *a day trip*

dead in the water (to be)
- *to be stopped; no progress*

deal breaker (a)
- *an issue that stops one or both parties from sealing a deal*

deductible
- *the amount a customer must pay before an insurance company will pay a claim*

deliver (to)
- *to perform as promised/expected*

demographic(s)
- *statistical characteristics of a population*

die for (to)
- *to desire at any cost*

dig in (to)
- *to start eating with great appetite*

dip into (to)
- *to steal from an account; to embezzle*

dirt (the)
- *gossip/rumor/scuttlebutt*

dirty laundry
- *embarrassing private business that becomes public*

discombobulated (to be)
- *to be confused/perplexed/flummoxed*

dismiss (to)
- *to let go/release from duties*

Ditto that.
- *I agree. Me too. You can say that again.*

division
- *department; section*

do something on the fly (to)
- *to do without preparation; to wing it*

doable (to be)
- *do + able; can be done; possible; manageable*

dog (a)
- *a bad idea; a poor performer*

dog-eat-dog world (a)
- *the strong eat the weak; the law of the jungle; no mercy*

done-deal (a)
- *a successful transaction*

Don't look a gift horse in the mouth.
- *Don't question the quality of a gift.*

dot one's i's and cross one's t's (to)
- *to check for detail errors; to go over with a fine-tooth comb*

double-down (to)
- *to double one's bet; to work twice as hard; to be more committed*

down-to-earth (to be)
- *to lack pretension; practical*

down to the wire (to be)
- *to be crunch time/zero hour as hard; to be more committed, etc.*

drag one's name through the mud (to)
- *to attack one's reputation publicly*

down-to-earth (to be)
- *to be practical/basic*

dressed to kill (to be)
- *to be dressed for success*

drive a hard bargain (to)
- *to make an offer too good to refuse*

driving at (to be)
- *to be making a point/aiming at*

drive home the point (to)
- *to emphasize/reinforce the message/issue/point, etc.*

drop everything (to)
- *to stop what one is doing*

drop the ball (to)
- *to fail to perform as expected*
drum up business (to)
- *to try and generate business*
due diligence
- *the investigation of facts before signing a contract*
D.U.I.
- *<u>d</u>riving <u>u</u>nder the <u>i</u>nfluence (of alcohol)*
dyed-in-the-wool (to be)
- *to be a true believer; unchangeable*

# E

earn one's stripes (to)
- *to demonstrate competency*
Earth to someone.
- *Hello? Are you awake/paying attention?*
eat crow (to)
- *to admit defeat/a mistake*
eat into something (to)
- *to drain away; to reduce slowly*
eat one's lunch (to)
- *to take away market share; to have a competitive edge*
eat out of one's hand (to)
- *to control/persuade easily*
eco-friendly (to be)
- *to be good for the environment*
economic bubble (an)
- *unjustified speculation that increases prices to unreasonable levels*
elaborate on something (to)
- *to develop in detail*
elevator pitch (an)
- *a 30-60 second argument delivered in the time it takes an elevator to go up; the summarizing of a product/service, etc. and its value proposition in a way that excites an audience*
end with a bang (to)
- *to finish with power/excitement*
entail (to)
- *to include/involve*
entity (an)
- *a thing that exists by itself; a business entity*

escrow account (an)
- *an account in which the monies of two parties is monitored by a third party*
euphemism (a)
- *a diplomatic word/comment replacing one that might offend/reflect* negatively
even playing field (an)
- *when the competition is equally matched*
exit strategy (an)
- *an exit plan; a way out*

# F

face the music (to)
- *to face reality/the truth*
face time
- *doing business face-to-face*
facing a budget crunch (to be)
- *to be anticipating operating under a limited budget; feeling the pinch*
fall off the face of the earth (to)
- *to disappear/vanish*
fall through the cracks (to)
- *to go by unnoticed only to become an issue later on*
falling out (a)
- *an argument/disagreement*
far cry from (to be a)
- *to be very different from*
fast-follower (a)
- *one that copies successful ideas and profits from them*
feedback
- *advice; constructive criticism*
feel like a fish out of water (to)
- *to feel lost/out of place*
feel the pinch (to)
- *to feel the effects of cost cutting*
fender bender (a)
- *a minor car accident*
figuratively speaking (to be)
- *to be speaking metaphorically*
final say (the)
- *the final word; the right to approve*
finer points (the)
- *the details*

finitiative
- *finish + initiative; having the initiative to finish/complete*

fire on all cylinders (to)
- *to work like a well-oiled engine*

fit in (to)
- *to belong*

fit the bill (to)
- *to be suitable; to match*

fixer-upper (a)
- *a listed residence needing work*

flea market (a)
- *an antique/used goods market*

flesh out something (to)
- *to develop/expand in detail*

flip (to)
- *to buy then immediately sell for a profit*

flip-flop (to)
- *to change one's position*

flood the market (to)
- *to oversupply a market with the same product*

fly (to)
- *to succeed*

fly by night (to)
- *to be here today, gone tomorrow; to be unreliable*

fly in the face of something (to)
- *to run contrary to*

fly on the wall (to be a)
- *to be a secret observer*

fly solo (to)
- *to go alone; a maverick*

flummoxed (to be)
- *to be confused/discombobulated*

follow in one's footstep's (to)
- *to do the same as one's parent*

for starters...
- *to start with; to begin with*

for the birds (to be)
- *to be a waste of time*

for the record
- *officially notified of the fact*

forfeiture
- *the loss of property as a result of default*

frank (to be)
- *to be honest/direct*

free ride (a)
- *a no-cost opportunity*

freebie (a)
- *a free promotional gift*

fringe benefits
- *incentives not included in a salary; bonus/perks*

from soup to nuts
- *controlling a process from start to finish*

from the ground up
- *from the lowest level up*

frugal (to be)
- *to be economical/thrifty/prudent*

fudge (to)
- *to fake/manipulate for positive results/gain*

fungible (to be)
- *to be interchangeable/substitutable*

# G

G (a)
- *a grand = one-thousand dollars; five-G's; ten-G's, etc.*

gender neutral (to be)
- *to favor neither sex; equal*

general counsel (the)
- *the lawyer who heads the legal department; also called the corporate counsel*

get buy-in (from someone) (to)
- *to get support/agreement*

get cold feet (to)
- *to become doubtful, reluctant*

get hung up (to)
- *to be delayed*

get more bang for one's buck (to)
- *to give more value for the price*

get on like a house on fire (to)
- *to get along very well*

get one's foot in the door (to)
- *to gain entry into a chosen place*

get one's walking papers (to)
- *to receive official notice of employment termination; to give one a pink slip*

get the axe (to)
- *to be fired; to get one's walking papers; to get a pink slip*

get the ball rolling (to)
- *to start the process*
get the show on the road (to)
- *to begin*
gibberish
- *meaningless words; nonsense*
gist (the)
- *a brief summary; the bottom line*
give feedback (to)
- *to give constructive criticism*
give one his/her walking papers (to)
- *to give one official notice of
employment termination; to give one
a pink slip; to fire/lay off someone*
give one kudos (to)
- *to give one credit; to congratulate*
give one more bang for one's buck (to)
- *to give more value for the price*
give one the head's up (to)
- *to warn; to alert*
give one the pitch (to)
- *to try and sell someone an idea*
give one the run-around (to)
- *to delay/avoid/frustrate*
give someone one's two cents (to)
- *to express one's opinion*
give the keynote (address) (to)
- *to give the main speech/talk*
give the-thumbs-down (to)
- *to reject/disapprove*
glass ceiling
- *an invisible male barrier that stops
females from advancing*
glib (to be)
- *to be superficial; lacking depth*
go back to square one (to)
- *to start over from the beginning*
go back to the drawing board (to)
- *to rethink; to start over*
go ballistic (to)
- *to explode with sudden anger*
go for a spin (to)
- *to go for a drive*
go for it (to)
- *to do something; to take action*
go hand-in-hand (to)
- *to go together; a logical connection*
go in one's stead (to)
- *to substitute/stand in for*

go national (to)
- *to enter the national market*
go off the rails (to)
- *to lose focus; to act strange*
go on a shopping spree (to)
- *to shop with no regard for cost*
go over with a fine-tooth comb (to)
- *to inspect carefully*
go overboard (to)
- *to try too hard*
go out on a limb (to)
- *to take a chance/risk*
go public (to)
- *to turn a private company into a
public company (corporation)*
go the extra mile (to)
- *to bend over backwards for
someone; to do more than is expected*
go through the roof (to)
- *to go ballistic or to reach an extreme
and unexpected height*
go to bat for someone (to)
- *to support a friend/colleague/
cause*
go to the ends of the earth (to)
- *to go to the extreme; to go the extra
mile for; to bend over backwards for*
go to town (to)
- *to spend/invest regardless of cost*
go your own way (to)
- *to march the beat of one's own
drummer*
golden parachute (a)
- *a well-funded retirement plan*
good egg (a)
- *a good person*
good for one's ego (to be)
- *to be good for one's self-esteem*
grab a chair (to)
- *to sit*
grab something (to)
- *to buy quickly*
grapevine (the)
- *the rumor mill*
grasp at straws (to)
- *to guess with no information*
Great Depression (the)
- *world economic depression,
circa 1930-1940*

green around the gills (to be)
- *to lack experience; a tyro*
green card (a)
- *in the U.S., a permanent-resident card which allows one to work legally*
green light (the)
- *the OK; the go-ahead; permission*
greentail (to)
- *to sell eco-friendly (green) products*
greentailing
- *the selling of eco-friendly products*
ground zero (to be)
- *to be the center of action*
Gulfstream (a)
- *upscale private jet*
gun for (to)
- *to go after with determination*

# H

half-baked (to be)
- *not complete; not serious or thought through*
handful (to be a)
- *to be problematic/hard to control*
hand it to someone (to)
- *to give someone credit/kudos*
hand over fist
- *done quickly in succession*
hang one's hat (to)
- *to take up residence; to be part of*
happy camper (to be not a)
- *a person who is not happy*
harbinger of... (to be a)
- *to be a sign/symbol that is a message foretelling future events*
hard nut to crack (a)
- *a problem difficult to solve/fix; a tough putt*
hard selling
- *appealing to consumer fears, greed, vanity; opposite of soft selling*
have a burr under one's saddle (to)
- *to have a reason to be annoyed*
have a feather in one's cap (to)
- *to have a distinctive achievement*
have a grasp of something (to)
- *to understand the task/issue*

have a knack for something (to)
- *to have a talent/affinity for*
have a leg to stand on (to not)
- *to have no argument/defense*
have a leg up on (to)
- *to have the advantage*
have a lot riding on something/ someone (to)
- *to depend on greatly*
have a meltdown (to)
- *to have a loss of emotional control*
have a mind of one's own (to)
- *to refuse to take orders*
have a monkey on one's back (to)
- *to carry a personal problem*
have a nose for something (to)
- *to have a talent/knack for*
have a notch on one's belt (to)
- *to have a feather in one's cap*
have a thick skin (to)
- *to be tough/resilient/resolute*
have all the bases covered (to)
- *to be prepared thoroughly*
have an exit strategy (to)
- *to have exit plan/way out*
have an eye for something (to)
- *to have a talent for*
have an in (to)
- *to have a connection with influence*
have an out (to)
- *to have an exit strategy/excuse*
have bigger fish to fry (to)
- *to have more profitable options*
have butterflies in one's stomach (to)
- *to be nervous*
have buyer's remorse (to)
- *to regret buying something*
have (get) cold feet (to)
- *to be nervous/reluctant/doubting*
have curb appeal (to)
- *to look desirable from the street*
have given one enough rope (to)
- *to have given one enough time/ chances*
have (got) what it takes (to)
- *to have the ability/talent to succeed*
have irons in the fire (to)
- *to have many ongoing plans that might be profitable*

have (got) it covered (to)
- *to take control/action*
have kittens (to)
- *to express extreme worry/fear*
have much (a lot) on one's plate, (to)
- *to have too much to do; overwhelmed*
have one's ducks in a row (to)
- *to be organized*
have one's finger on the button (to)
- *to be in a position to control events*
have someone in your corner (to)
- *to have the help/support of one from whom you will benefit*
have the upper hand (to)
- *to have the advantage*
have to inherit a reservation (to)
- *to wait forever to get a reservation*
have wiggle room (to)
- *to have room to negotiate; to be flexible*
have zero tolerance for something (to)
- *to have no room for unethical behavior*
head up something (to)
- *to manage/run a company, charity, school, etc.*
headhunter (a)
- *a job recruiter*
heads up (the)
- *the information/warning/notice*
heavy hitter (a)
- *a person with power and influence; an A-player; a big gun/top dog*
here's the deal...
- *this is the bottom line...*
hiccups
- *problems*
high-fructose corn syrup
- *low-cost, calorie-rich sweetener made from corn; used in fast-food*
high time
- *about time; time to act*
hired gun (a)
- *a specialist brought in to fix a problem*
hit (a)
- *a financially successful product*
hit all the right notes (to)
- *to say/do everything right; perfect*

hit and miss (to be)
- *to be irregular in quality/outcome*
hit it out of the park (to)
- *to hit a homerun; to succeed; to think of a great idea; to succeed beyond expectation*
hit the gas (to)
- *to go faster; to work harder*
hit the glass ceiling (to)
- *to hit an invisible male barrier that stops females from advancing*
hit the ground running (to)
- *to do immediately and quickly, adjusting to conditions as one goes*
hit the jackpot (to)
- *to win the big prize*
hit the panic button (to)
- *to lose emotional control; to freak out*
hit the reset button (to)
- *to go back to the drawing board; to rethink; to reboot a computer*
hit the roof (to)
- *to be very upset/angry; to go ballistic*
hit the wall (to)
- *to have run out of energy*
hold all the cards (to)
- *to be in the best position to win/gain*
hold something (to)
- *to not include; to leave off/out*
hold water (to not)
- *to lack persuasiveness*
homestretch (the)
- *the final part/phase of a project*
hook someone/something (to)
- *to get/obtain/hire*
hook up (with) (to)
- *to meet (with)*
hooked (to be)
- *to be interested/curious to know more*
hot-button issue (a)
- *a controversial topic*
hound (to)
- *to bother; to go after continually*
howl at the moon (to)
- *to believe the impossible is doable; crazy*

hypoallergenic (to be)
- *to be non allergenic*

# I

I take it (that)...
- *I assume (that)...*

icing on the cake (the)
- *the best part; the added benefit*

If it ain't (isn't) broke (broken), don't fix it.
- *Why mess with success? Why change a winning plan?*

If the shoe fits, wear it.
- *If it works, do it/go for it.*

I'll get back to you on that one.
- *I'm not interested/not impressed; I don't think so.*

I'm all ears.
- *I'm listening. Shoot.*

in a New-York minute
- *instantly; immediately*

in a nut shell
- *in brief; in short*

in a pinch (to be)
- *to be in a situation in which a substitute is the only alternative*

in a quandary (to be)
- *in a state of confusion/doubt*

in light of...
- *considering the fact that...*

in line for something (to be)
- *to be next in line for something*

in one's corner
- *on one's side/team*

in one's sights (to be)
- *to be aiming at a target/goal in for*

in the bag (to be)
- *to be guaranteed*

in the ballpark (to be)
- *to be approximate; within range*

in the black (to be)
- *to be showing a profit/gain*

in the doghouse (to be)
- *to be out of favor; under a cloud*

in the long run
- *over a long period of time*

in the loop (to be)
- *to be in the circle of communication; connected*

in the market for (to be)
- *to be looking to buy or rent*

in the pipeline (to be)
- *to be in the development process*

in the public eye (to be)
- *to be open for all to see/review, etc.*

in the red (to be)
- *to be showing a loss; in debt; negative*

in this neck of the woods
- *in this neighborhood/town/city*

in too deep (to be)
- *to be too involved to exit without a loss*

in turn
- *as a result; it follows*

incentive (an)
- *a reason to perform, i.e., a bonus*

incur (to)
- *to take on; to take possession of*

inventory
- *a list of goods/property on hand to support production /sales, etc.*

IPO
- *initial public offering; the first day shares of a new public company are sold to the public*

iron fist in a velvet glove (an)
- *to be diplomatic yet strict*

iron out something (to)
- *to correct/fix/resolve*

itching to do something (to be)
- *impatiently waiting to proceed*

It's a dog-eat-dog world.
- *everyone for themselves; no mercy*

It's money in the bank.
- *a safe bet; guaranteed*

It's not what you know, but who you know.
- *connections are better than knowledge when seeking gain*

## J

Joe (a cup of)
- *a cup of coffee; java; caffeine*

jog one's memory (to)
- *to help someone remember*

jump all over someone (to)
- *to confront/attack without warning*

jump at the chance (to)
- *to accept immediately*

jump out of the frying pan and into the fire (to)
- *to move from a bad position to one that is worse*

jump ship (to)
- *to leave suddenly*

jump the gun (to)
- *to rush to a wrong conclusion; to start too early*

jump the shark (to)
- *the moment when something successful begins to fail; the beginning of the end*

jump through the hoops (to)
- *to face many obstacles to reach a goal*

jumpy (to be)
- *to be nervous/edgy/stressed*

just for starters
- *just the beginning*

just for the record
- *to clarify one's position; this idiom is often used informally as a way of reminding one of a time/event/ opinion, etc.*

Just say the word.
- *Just say okay. Just tell me when.*

## K

keep an open mind (to)
- *to be understanding; to not prejudge*

keeper (a)
- *a lover/spouse one should keep/hold on to*

keep it on the up-and-up (to)
- *to be professional/ethical*

keep one's eye on the prize (to)
- *to stay focused on one's goal*

keep one's fingers crossed (to)
- *to hope for the best; pray*

keep one's head above water (to)
- *to manage; to survive*

keep one's shirt on (to)
- *to settle down/relax/be patient*

kerfuffle (a)
- *a disagreement/commotion/fuss*

kick (to be a)
- *to be fun/great/a blast*

kick it up a notch (to)
- *to take something to the next level*

kick off (to)
- *to start*

kick oneself (to)
- *to blame oneself*

kick oneself for the rest of one's life (to)
- *to regret always*

kick something around (to)
- *to discuss/brainstorm*

kill to do something/be someone (to)
- *to do anything to attain/become*

killer app (a)
- *a computer application (software) that makes a computer worth owning*

killer instinct
- *a ruthless desire to succeed/win*

knock [number] percent off (to)
- *to reduce by the stated percentage*

knock one's socks off (to)
- *to impress greatly; to amaze*

Knock yourself out.
- *Go ahead. Go for it. No problem.*

kudos
- *congratulations/credit*

## L

labor of love (a)
- *done for love not money or gain*

land someone (to)
- *to hire*

land something (to)
- *to get/win something*

last straw (the)

- *the moment when the line has been crossed*

laundry list (a)
- *a to-do list*

lay it on the line (to)
- *to speak frankly/honestly*

lay one's cards on the table (to)
- *to speak frankly; to state the bottom line; to lay it on the line*

learn the ropes (to)
- *to learn the system*

leave well enough alone (to)
- *to not touch*

lend a hand (to)
- *to offer help*

let the chips fall where they may (to)
- *to let fate/destiny decide*

letter of intent (a) (LOI)
- *a letter outlining an agreement between two parties written before they seal the deal*

liable (to be)
- *to be legally responsible/obligated*

lien (a)
- *a legal claim on a property*

lift (a)
- *a ride*

like a cat on a hot tin roof (to be)
- *to be nervous/jumpy*

limited partnership (a)
- *a business that combines the features of a corporation and a partnership for tax shelter purposes*

list (to)
- *to put a property on the market*

little girl's/boy's room (the)
- *the women's/men's restroom*

Location, location, location.
- *real estate rule #1*

locavore (a)
- *one who supports local farmers*

long shot (a)
- *having little or no chance of success*

look as nervous as a cat in a room full of rocking chairs (to)
- *to look nervous/scared/jumpy*

look good on paper (to)
- *to work in theory*

look like the cat that ate the canary (to)

- *to look self-satisfied/pleased*

lose one's shirt (to)
- *to experience a significant loss*

lose one's touch (to)
- *to lose the ability to do something*

lottery (the green card)
- *the Diversity Immigrant Visa Lottery; U.S. government lottery that awards 50,000 green cards annually*

love at first sight (to be)
- *to feel an instant attraction for*

low hanging fruit
- *opportunities that can be readily obtained*

luck out (to)
- *to get lucky*

luxurious (to be)
- *to be the finest/best/upscale*

# M

Madison Avenue
- *a main north-south avenue in Manhattan, NYC; where the modern advertising business started, circa 1920; traditionally the center of the advertising business*

make a fuss (to)
- *to argue/complain; to worry about*

make amends (to)
- *to compensate for negligent behavior*

make a mountain out of a molehill (to)
- *to make something bigger/worse than it is*

make a splash (to)
- *to make a favorable impression*

make-over (a)
- *a change of image; a new look*

making money is the name of the game
- *in the business world (game), making money is all that matters*

man up (to)
- *to act like a man; be brave/strong*

march to the beat of one's own drummer (to)
- *to be an individual; to go your own way; to fly solo*

marching orders
  - *instructions from a superior*
margin of error (the)
  - *the amount of allowable error*
marketing mix
  - *the 4Ps of a marketing plan:*
  *product, price, place, promotion*
maverick (a)
  - *a rebel; a lone wolf; one who flies*
  *solo*
meet-and-greet (a)
  - *a first meeting*
me-too product (a)
  - *a product copied after a bestseller*
meltdown (a)
  - *a loss of emotional control*
mettle
  - *strength of character; will*
Mickey-D's
  - *McDonald's*
miffed (to be)
  - *to be upset/angry/peeved*
mince words (to)
  - *to avoid the truth*
modus operandi (Latin)
  - *MO; method of operation; the way*
  *of doing something*
monopoly (a)
  - *producers controlling a market*
moonlighting (to be)
  - *to be working off hours tax-free*
MOR
  - *middle-of-the-road; typical; average*
moratorium (Latin)
  - *an official waiting period in which*
  *amendments are sought or made*
motto (a)
  - *a short statement expressing a*
  *belief or purpose*
mouthwatering (to be)
  - *to look delicious/appetizing*
move the goal posts (to)
  - *the arbitrary changing of rules often*
  *to serve a losing side*
mover and a shaker (a)
  - *one with power and influence*
movers and shakers
  - *those with power and influence*
mull something over (to)
  - *to think about; to consider carefully*

Mum's the word
- *Keep it secret.*
my hands are tied
- *I have no freedom to control or influence.*
my way or the highway
- *an ultimatum; do as I say or game over; ship up or shape out*
myriad
- *many; a lot of*

# N

nail something (to)
- *to get it right; to succeed*
nail something down (to)
- *to finish/finalize*
name-dropper (a)
- *one who tries to gain advantage by mentioning influential names*
name of the game (the)
- *the purpose of one's business*
natural (a)
- *one with innate/natural talent*
navigate the system (to)
- *to know how to work within a system; to know the ropes*
need something like one needs a hole in the head (to)
- *to have neither need nor desire for*
negligent (to be)
- *failure to exercise care/caution*
nest-egg (a)
- *long-term personal retirement savings*
nevertiree (a)
- *one who will never retire*
new blood
- *new employees; new talent*
new normal (the)
- *the new standard/practice*
niche market (a)
- *a small specialized market*
nickel-and-dime one (to)
- *to be cheap/stingy/tight-fisted*
night owl (a)
- *one who prefers the night*
nitty-gritty (the)
- *the details; the basic facts*

No fooling.
- *Is that right? No kidding.*
no free lunch (there is)
- *nothing is free*
no ifs, ands or buts
- *no excuses*
no-name something (a)
- *a non brand name; a generic brand*
no one can hold a candle to someone/something...
- *no competition; no equal*
no sweat
- *no problem*
not be in one's vocabulary (to)
- *ironic emphasis used when stating one's opinion; any noun can be used, for example: Hate is not in my vocabulary; Failure is not...; Meat is not...; Vacation is not..., etc.*
not my cup of tea (to be)
- *not for me; not a preference*
nothing if not predictable (to be)
- *to be predictable*
Nothing is set in stone.
- *not finalized; not guaranteed*
Nothing to write home about.
- *nothing special/important*
nouveau riche (to be)
- *French for the new rich; to be rich in one's own generation*
Now we're talking.
- *All right. Great idea!*
nuts about something/someone (to be)
- *to be crazy about*
nuts and bolts (the)
- *the basics/fundamentals*
NYSE (the)
- *the New York Stock Exchange*

# O

obstacle (an)
- *a barrier/challenge*
of a mind to... (to be)
- *to be inclined to...*
of two minds (to be)
- *to be considering two positions at the same time*

off one's rocker (to be)
- *to be crazy/eccentric/unpredictable*
off something (to be)
- *no longer doing/eating something*
old boys' club (an)
- *a traditional club only men can join; an organization that lacks gender-neutrality*
old flame (an)
- *ex lover*
old hand at something (to be an)
- *to have a lot of experience doing something*
old money (to be)
- *to be historically wealthy*
oligarchy (an)
- *a corrupt government controlled by a few for self gain*
on a roll (to be)
- *to experience a series of successes*
on an ego trip (to be)
- *to be blowing one's horn ad nauseum*
on board (to be)
- *to be part of a plan; to be participating;*
on cloud nine (to be)
- *to feel fantastic*
on fire (to be)
- *to have a series of successes/hits*
on tap
- *beer poured at the bar from a tap*
on the block (to be)
- *to be available for purchase; on the market*
on the chopping block (to be)
- *to be in serious trouble*
on the dot
- *at the exact specified time*
on the market (to be)
- *to be available for purchase; on the block*
on the line (to be)
- *to be calling on the phone*
on the line (to be)
- *when something is facing possible possible loss/damage, etc.*
on the same page (to be)
- *to be in agreement; to see eye-to-eye*

on the set (to be)
- *to be present at the location where a movie or photo shoot is taking place*
on (the right) track (to be)
- *to be moving in the right direction on time*
once in a blue moon
- *rarely*
only game in town (the)
- *the only/best choice*
open a can of worms (to)
- *to create more problems while trying to solve one problem*
open with a bang (to)
- *to start with power/excitement*
optics
- *how the public views an issue/product/decision, etc.*
out (an)
- *an exit strategy; a way out*
out of favor (to be)
- *to be in the doghouse*
out of one's league (to be)
- *to beyond one's reach/abilities*
out of the woods (to be)
- *to be out of danger*
outrageous (to be)
- *to be unbelievable/shocking*
outsider (an)
- *a rebel; one who marches to the beat of one's own drum*
overflow (to)
- *to spill over due to excess volume; to burst at the seams*
overhaul (an)
- *a rebuilding/redesigning to improve*
overhaul (to)
- *to rebuild/redesign to improve*
overwhelmed (to be)
- *overpowered by work/emotion, etc.*

# P

pan something (to)
- *to reject with severe criticism*
paper over (to)
- *to hide/cover up*
paper tiger (a)

*- to appear strong when weak in fact*

paradigm shift (a)
  *- a change in basic assumptions*
paragon (a)
  *- one who is a model of excellence;
  the best example*
parked on the other [phone] line (to
be)
  *- to be placed on hold*
pass the buck (to)
  *- to avoid responsibility by giving it to
  someone else*
pat on the back (a)
  *- congratulations/ kudos*
peddle (to)
  *- to sell/ promote/ pitch*
pencil one in (to)
  *- to schedule an appointment*
  penthouse (a)
  *- luxury apartment on the top floor*
perks
  *- benefits*
per se
  *- in and of itself*
perplexed (to be)
  *- confused/ discombobulated*
pick one's brain (to)
  *- to ask a series of questions for
  clarification/ feedback*
piece of cake (a)
  *- no problem; as easy as pie*
pied-à-terre (French)
  *- "foot on the ground"; temporary or
  secondary lodging*
pile up (to)
  *- to grow large in size/ volume*
pinch hit (to)
  *- to substitute for; to stand in for*
pinch hitter (a)
  *- a substitute for someone*
pinch pennies (to)
  *- to live frugally; to control costs by
  limiting expenses*
pink slip (a)
  *- a traditional official notice of
  employment termination; walking
  papers*
piping hot (to be)
  *- to be fresh out of oven*
pitch (a)
  *- a short persuasive argument*

pitch (to)
- *to deliver a brief argument aimed at selling an idea/product*

pitchman (a)
- *one who sells (pitches) ideas; a product spokesperson*

pitfall (a)
- *a problem, potential or actual*

pizza joint (a)
- *a small restaurant specializing in pizza*

play by the book (to)
- *to follow the rules/law*

play favorites (to)
- *to show preference/bias*

play with fire (to)
- *to take extreme risks*

plug (to)
- *to pitch a product/idea; to advertise*

poised to take someone/something to the next level (to be)
- *to be in a position to move up to the next level of service/expertise/competition, etc.*

pony up (to)
- *to pay what is owed/needed*

portfolio (a)
- *a group of financial investments*

pound the pavement (to)
- *to go and look for work/customers*

powder one's nose (to)
- *to freshen up in the women's restroom*

preach to the choir (to)
- *to try and persuade an audience that already supports/agrees with you*

price fix (to)
- *competitors agreeing to the same price*

price oneself out of the market (to)
- *to raise/keep a price so high that consumers look for lower prices, the result being a loss of market share*

prick up (to)
- *to stand up*

product pipeline
- *products a company has in development*

productivity study (a)
- *a statistical measure of worker production over time*

profit
- *financial benefit realized when revenue exceeds expenses*

promote from within (to)
- *to promote in-house employees*

prospects
- *chances of success*

prototype (a)
- *a test model*

PSF
- *price per square foot*

psyched (to be)
- *to be full of enthusiasm and excitement*

pull a rabbit out of the hat (to)
- *to perform magic/a miracle*

pull an all-nighter (to)
- *to work all night*

pull one's punches (to)
- *to mince words; to avoid speaking critically/frankly*

pull oneself up by one's bootstraps (to)
- *to improve one's situation by one's own efforts*

pull out all the stops (to)
- *to do whatever is necessary to succeed*

pull something off (to)
- *to do/achieve*

pull the plug (on) (to)
- *to stop a process*

pull the wool over one's eyes (to)
- *to fool/deceive someone*

pull up one's socks (to)
- *to self-improve through hard work*

push one's buttons (to)
- *to cause one to become annoyed/angry*

pushing paper (to be)
- *to be doing routine office work*

pushover (to be a)
- *one who is easily persuaded*

put a fire under it (to)
- *to hurry up; to get moving*

put in an appearance (to)
- *to show up*

put into layman's language (to)
- *to explain in simple (non expert) English*

put one's nose to the grindstone (to)
- *to work hard*

put oneself in another's shoes (to)
- *to consider from a new/different perspective*

put someone through (to)
- *to connect one to another by phone line*

put the pedal to the metal (to)
- *to hit the gas; to take action quickly*

# Q

quid pro quo (Latin)
- *something for something*

# R

rainmaker (a)
- *a money-maker*

raise (a)
- *a salary or wage increase*

raise Cain (to)
- *to cause trouble*

rake something in (to)
- *to collect in large amounts*

ramp up (to)
- *to increase in speed*

ready for prime time (to be)
- *to be ready to step up to the plate; to be ready to be presented/sold to the public on prime-time TV, the hours between 8:00-10:30 p.m. when the largest audience is watching*

red-eye (the)
- *any midnight flight*

redress
- *compensation*

red tape
- *excessive official rules limiting/ stopping progress*

rein in something (to)
- *to reduce/limit by strict control*

rep (a)
- *a representative*

rest on one's laurels (to)
- *to depend on one's reputation with no further effort*

résumé (French)
- *curriculum vitae*

retreat to the suburbs (to)
- *to retire/move to the suburbs*

revenue
- *income generated from sales and services before deductions*

ride on one's coattails (to)
- *to succeed not by ability but by connections*

RIFed (to be)
- *a reduction in force; to be laid off to reduce the number of employees due to a lack of work/money/ reorganization, etc.*

right on the button (to be)
- *to be exact/correct/spot on*

right under one's nose (to be)
- *to be so close you cannot see it*

road warrior (a)
- *one who is always traveling for business*

roll up one's sleeves (to)
- *to get serious and work harder*

roll with the punches (to)
- *to deal with challenges as they appear*

rolling in it (to be)
- *to be rolling in money; rich/wealthy*

rub elbows (with) (to)
- *to socialize with; to schmooze*

rub it in (to)
- *to tease by always reminding*

rub someone the wrong way (to)
- *to annoy/upset/anger*

rubberneck (to)
- *to slow down and look at an accident*

rule with an iron fist (to)
- *to control with absolute authority*

ruminate (to)
- *to mull it over; to think about*

rumor has it (that)...
- *the rumor is (that)...; the buzz is...*

rumormonger (a)
- *one who spreads rumors; a gossip*

run a tight ship (to)
- *to manage efficiently; disciplined*

run-down (a)
- *a report/update*

run-of-the-mill (to be)
- *to be regular/typical/M.O.R.*

run oneself ragged (to)
- *to exhaust oneself in an extreme way*

run something by someone (to)
- *to present for approval/feedback*

Run that by me again.
- *Please tell me again.*

run the numbers (to)
- *to do financial calculations; to crunch the numbers*

run through something (to)
- *to review/explain*

run with the big boys (to)
- *to go big; to swim with the sharks*

# S

sacred cow (a)
- *untouchable; cannot be criticized*

sacrifice (to)
- *to give up something in order for another to benefit*

saddled with something (to be)
- *to be forced to carry a big load/responsibility*

salt of the earth (the)
- *one who is ethical/down-to-earth*

scale back one's hours (to)
- *to reduce one's working hours*

scarf down (to)
- *to eat with great appetite; to wolf down*

schmooze (to)
- *to socialize for personal gain*

schmoozer (a)
- *one who socializes for personal gain; one who likes to rub elbows*

scratch
- *money*

scratch pad (a)
- *a note pad*

screw up (to)
- *to blow it; to make a big mistake*

scuttlebutt (the)
- *the latest rumor(s)/gossip*

seal the deal (to)
- *to come to an agreement*

second-to-none (to be)
- *to be the best; without equal*

securities company (a)
- *a company that sells financial products, such as stocks and bonds*

see eye-to-eye (to)
- *to be on the same page; to agree*

sell oneself short (to)
- *to not believe in yourself/abilities*

sell out to someone/thing (to)
- *to go against one's beliefs/ policies for financial gain*

seller's market (a)
- *a market in which sellers can set the price due to limited inventory*

send the right/wrong vibe (to)
- *to send the right/wrong message*

sentimental (to be)
- *to be emotional*

set off (to)
- *to leave*

set one back (to)
- *to be put into the red*

set one up with someone (to)
- *to arrange to have a meeting with someone*

set one's sights a little lower/higher (to)
- *to reduce/increase expectations based on one's abilities/resources, etc.*

set up shop (in) (to)
- *to open a business (in)*

shape up or ship out (to)
- *to perform or leave; my way or the highway; ultimatum*

share (a)
- *a stock; financial paper*

shareholder (a)
- *one who owns stock in a company*

shareholders meeting (a)
- *annual meeting in which a public company speaks to its shareholders*

shark (a)
- *a take-no-prisoners player*

shingle (a)
- *traditionally a wooden sign advertising a law practice*

shoe-in (a)
- *a definite winner*

shoe is on the other foot (the)
- *the tables have been turned*

shoe-string budget (a)
- *a budget set as low as possible*

Shoot.
- *Go ahead. I'm all ears.*

shoot (a)
- *a photo shoot; when products/ models are photographed*

shoot down in flames (to)
- *to throw cold water on*

shoot oneself in the foot (to)
- *to do/say something that negatively effects oneself*

shop around (to)
- *to look for a better deal*

shopping spree (a)
- *shopping with no regard for cost*

short-term costs
- *current expenses*

shot (a)
- *a chance*

shot in the arm (a)
- *a stimulus; inspiration*

sign on the dotted line (to)
- *to sign a contract; to seal the deal*

sign someone (to)
- *to sign a contract; to cut a deal*

sink the ship (to)
- *to destroy/negatively impact a business*

sit in the catbird seat (to)
- *to be sitting pretty*

sit on it (to)
- *to take no action*

sit on the fence (to)
- *to make no decision either way*

sitting duck (a)
- *an easy target*

sitting pretty (to be)
- *to be in an advantageous position*

size up (to)
- *to inspect in detail*

skedaddle (to)
- *to leave/go*

skill set
- *one's abilities/talents/expertise*

skinny on (the)
- *the basic facts about something; the latest news*

sky is the limit (the)
- *unlimited opportunities*

slam-dunk (a)
- *a sure thing*

slave driver (a)
- *a superior with no compassion; dictator*

slave over something (to)
- *to work at continually with slow progress*

slave to something (to be a)
- *to have a strong desire for; addicted*

sleep on it (to)
- *to consider and make a decision at a later date*

sleeper (a)
- *a product that becomes a hit due to word-of-mouth advertising*

slice of the pie (a)
- *a piece of the market/action*

slip one's mind (to)
- *to forget*

slipshod (to be)
- *to be of poor quality*

small potatoes (to be)
- *to be insignificant/minor*

smoking gun (a)
- *evidence of a crime/guilt*

snag something (to)
- *to land/get/win/hook*

snowed under (to be)
- *to be swamped/overwhelmed*

soft selling
- *appealing to consumer needs and wants; opposite of hard selling*

soirée (French)
- *an evening party*

sole proprietorship (a)
- *a business in which one assumes all the risks and benefits; a sole proprietor*

solutioning
- *problem + solution; finding a solution to a problem*

sound divine (to)
- *to sound like heaven/perfect*

sound like a broken record (to)
- *to repeat again and again*

Sounds like a plan.
- *Sounds like a good idea.*

speak one's language (to)
- *to communicate using the vocabulary of one's audience/ market*

spin (to)
- *to present information favorably to gain the advantage*

spin doctor (a)
- *one who favorably promotes the actions/opinions of an individual/ organization*

spin off (a)
- *a product(s) developed from a successful product*

spin one's wheels (to)
- *to lack progress; to be stopped*

spin someone/something in a positive light (to)
- *to describe favorably in a way that runs contrary to the evidence*

spot (a)
- *a commercial; a 30-second spot, a 60-second spot, etc.*

squeeze in a look (at) (to)
- *to make time to see something*

stand to gain (to)
- *to benefit from*

stand to lose (to)
- *to face possible loss*

start from scratch (to)
- *to start with basic resources*

starving (to be)
- *to be very hungry*

state of the art (to be)
- *to be the best design/technology, etc., available at the time*

status quo (the) (Latin)
- *the current situation/state of affairs*

staycation (a)
- *a stay-at-home vacation*

steal (a)
- *a product with a low price; a bargain*

steal a march on (to)
- *to arrive before another; to gain the advantage due to a quick first move*

step up to the plate (to)
- *to take action/responsibility*

stick to one's guns (to)
- *to hold one's position; to refuse to budge*

stickler for detail (to be a)
- *one who demands perfection*

sticker shock
- *the shock received from the high price on a sales tag*

stimulus
- *something that stimulates; a shot in the arm*

stock (a)
- *a financial instrument; a piece of paper representing partial ownership of a public company*

stodgy (to be)
- *to be old-fashioned/conservative*

straight shooter (a)
- *one who is honest/frank*

strapped for something (to be)
- *to be low on something; to have no extra money/time, etc.*

straw that broke the camel's back (the)
- *The last act in a series of unacceptable acts.*

strawman argument (a)
- *misrepresenting an opponent's position with false claims; informal fallacy*

strike while the iron is hot (to)
- *to do immediately to gain the advantage*

strip mall (a)
- *retail stores located near intersections*

stroke one's ego (to)
- *to flatter; to butter up*

stuck in traffic (to be)
- *to be in a vehicle but not moving due to heavy traffic/accident, etc.*

stuffed shirt (a)
- *a buttoned-down person who believes he/she is superior*

sue (to)
- *to take legal action for redress*
sue for compensation (to)
- *to sue for money owed*
suffer fools lightly (to not)
- *to have no patience for stupidity*
suffice (to)
- *to satisfy; to be enough*
suffice it to say (to)
- *in short; briefly; basically; to make a long story short*
sugarcoat (to)
- *to make something more appealing than it actually is*
suit (a)
- *a businessperson*
surrender (to)
- *to give up/capitulate; to throw in the towel*
swamped (with something) (to be)
- *to be overwhelmed with work*
sweeten the deal (to)
- *to make an offer more attractive by adding an incentive*
swim with the sharks (to)
- *to work with heavy hitters; to run with the big boys*
swing something (to)
- *to manage/achieve/resolve*
symbol (a)
- *a sign with meaning*

# T

tagline (a)
- *a slogan*
tailgater (a)
- *a driver following dangerously close behind*
tainted (to be)
- *to be infected/contaminated/corrupted*
take a bath (to)
- *to incur a large loss on an investment*
take a calculated risk (to)
- *to risk after assessing the odds*
take a crack at something (to)
- *to attempt/try*

take a rain check (to)
- *to promise to do another time*
take advantage of someone/ something (to)
- *to exploit for gain*
take no prisoners (to)
- *to show no mercy; no compromise*
take off (to)
- *to go up; to do well/succeed*
take one for a ride (to)
- *to take advantage of; to cheat*
take one for the team (to)
- *literally to take a bullet to protect others; to sacrifice oneself for the common good*
take one to the cleaners (to)
- *to overcharge/rip off*
take out a bank loan (to)
- *to get a bank loan*
take something to the next level (to)
- *to go up a level in service / expertise*
take the bull by the horns (to)
- *to accept a difficult challenge*
take the high road (to)
- *to do what is best/honest/ethical*
take the reins (to)
- *to take control; to manage*
take the words right out of one's mouth (to)
- *to say what another is thinking*
take to the bank (to)
- *to profit from; you can take that to the bank.*
taken to the cleaners (to be)
- *to be overcharged/ripped off*
talk out of both sides of one's mouth (to)
- *to contradict oneself*
talk the talk and walk the walk (to)
- *the ability to put words into action*
talk through one's hat (to)
- *to sound like an expert when one is not*
tank (to)
- *to go down; to fail*
tasked with (to be)
- *to be assigned to*
taskmaster (a)
- *a slave driver*

tax write-off (a)
- *a tax benefit*
test the waters (to)
- *to test/try before committing*
tête-à-tête (French)
- *"head-to-head"; a private two-person meeting*
that close to...
- *just about to do something*
That said...
- *Knowing that...; In light of that...*
the deal is on the line...
- *the deal is waiting to be signed/ agreed upon; the deal is at risk*
the story of my life...
- *that is what always happens to me*
the upside is...
- *the advantage is...*
the wheels fell off something when...
- *the point when everything went wrong; a negative turning point*
tied up (to be)
- *to be busy/not available*
think outside the box (to)
- *to think differently/originally*
This place is you all over.
- *This place suits you perfectly.*
through the roof (to be)
- *to be extremely expensive/ emotional*
throw cold water on something (to)
- *to reject with criticism*
throw in something (to)
- *to include at no extra cost*
throw in the towel (to)
- *to give up/surrender/capitulate*
throw one a curve (to)
- *to introduce something that is new and unexpected*
throw one under the bus (to)
- *to sacrifice someone/thing for gain*
throw one's hat in the ring (to)
- *to enter/join*
throw the baby out with the bath water (to)
- *when eliminating a negative, a positive element is also lost; an avoidable error*
tie the knot (to)
- *to get married*

tight-fisted (to be)
- *to be miserly/frugal/cheap*
TLC
- *tendering-loving care*
to the tune of... (to be)
- *to the amount of...*
total package (the)
- *the perfect mix; all included*
totally
- *definitely/absolutely*
touch all bases (to)
- *to cover everything; to hit all the right notes*
touch-and-go (to be)
- *to be uncertain/in doubt*
touch base with someone (to)
- *to meet/contact someone*
tough call (a)
- *a difficult decision; a tough putt*
tough putt (a)
- *a difficult golf shot; a challenge*
trace (to)
- *to find/locate*
track down (to)
- *to research; to try and find*
track record (a)
- *a history of past performance*
traffic jam (a)
- *a delay caused by heavy traffic*
transition into something (to)
- *to change from one to another*
trash (to)
- *to criticize severely*
trashed (to be)
- *to be severely criticized*
tread water (to)
- *to swim in one place; to lack progress; to spin one's wheels*
trendsetter (a)
- *one who starts a trend; an original thinker who is imitated*
trial balloon (a)
- *a test to measure a reaction*
trip the light fantastic (to)
- *to dance/party all night long*
trust-fund (a)
- *legal holding containing assets benefiting an individual/organization*

trust-fund baby (a)
- *rich from inheriting a trust fund*
turn a profit (to)
- *to make a profit*
turn the tables (to)
- *to reverse positions and gain the advantage*
twenty-questions
- *a game in which one asks another twenty questions as clues to finding an answer/secret, etc.*
twist (a)
- *an unexpected/surprise ending to a movie/story/event, etc.*
tyro (a)
- *a beginner/newbie/neophyte; one who is green around the gills*

## U

ultimatum (an)
- *an either-or proposition*
under a cloud (to be)
- *to be viewed negatively; to be out of a favor/in the doghouse*
under the gun (to be)
- *to be under great pressure*
underwrite something (to)
- *to support financially*
unload something (to)
- *to sell something*
up-and-comer (an)
- *one with excellent prospects*
up for this (to be)
- *to be ready/prepared to do*
up the ante (to)
- *to take on more risk by increasing a bet; to increase the pressure*
up to scratch (to be)
- *to be done properly as required*
upmarket (to be)
- *to be luxurious/expensive/upscale*
upscale (to be)
- *to be upmarket*
unsurpassed (to be)
- *to be without equal; the best*

## V

value proposition (a)
- *a statement summarizing why a product/service will add value/solve a problem better than others; a brand's promise to perform*
vegan (a)
- *a vegetarian who does not eat dairy products*
vegan
- *a dairy-free (no eggs, milk, butter, cheese, yogurt etc.) diet*
vote of confidence (a)
- *a sign of support/approval*

## W

waffle (to)
- *to flip flop; to hesitate when faced with a choice; indecisive*
wait for the other shop to drop (to)
- *to wait for more bad news*
wait until the cows come home (to)
- *to wait for a very long time*
wake up to the fact that (to)
- *to realize*
Waldorf-Astoria, The
- *upscale hotel on Park Avenue beside Grand Central Station, NYC*
walk-up (a)
- *apartment or house with no elevator*
walking papers
- *employment termination notice; a pink slip*
wash-out (a)
- *a failure; a disappointment*
water down (to)
- *to reduce in strength*
water off a duck's back (to be)
- *to be easy; to have no effect*
water under the bridge
- *a past event that cannot be revisited; What's done is done (S).*
watering hole (a)
- *a restaurant/bar one visits regularly*
weather the storm (to)
- *to survive a difficult/challenging event*

weigh in on something (to)
- *to give one's opinion*
Well, I'll be.
- *Is that right? No fooling.*
What on earth?
- *What is going on? What are you doing?*
What's shaking in your world?
- *What's new?*
wheel and deal (to)
- *to negotiate; to bargain hard*
when pigs fly...
- *impossible; unlikely*
when push comes to shove...
- *when words become action*
when the chips are down...
- *when one feels defeated; when one is at a low point*
when word gets out (that)...
- *when many learn of the fact...*
white collar
- *management; white shirt and tie*
white-elephant (a)
- *property that sits empty because it will not sell due to price/ location, etc.*
whole different kettle of fish (to be a)
- *to be completely different; a whole different story*
whole different story (to be a)
- *to be completely different; a whole different kettle of fish*
whole nine yards (the)
- *everything; from soup to nuts*
who's who of something/somewhere (a)
- *the best of the best from...*
Why mess with success?
- *Why change a winning game plan?*
wicked (to be)
- *to be bad or good depending on the context*
win hands down (to)
- *to win decisively*
wing it (to)
- *to do on the fly; to improvise*
wishy-washy (to be)
- *to be uncertain/undecided*

wiz at something (to be a)
- *to be a wizard; one with special talent*
wolf down (to)
- *to scarf down*
wolf in sheep's clothing (a)
- *one who appears harmless but is in fact ruthless/dangerous*
wolf is at the door (the)
- *the threat of becoming poor*
wolves are at the door (the)
- *people impatiently waiting to take action*
word-of-mouth advertising
- *satisfied customers recommending a product/service to friends*
work a/the room (to)
- *to schmooze*
work down to the wire (to)
- *to work to the last minute*
work-life balance
- *the balance between work and family life*
work out the kinks (to)
- *to find and solve problems*
work something through (to)
- *to find a solution to a problem*
work up something (to)
- *to develop ideas; to brainstorm*
works (the)
- *everything*
working lunch (a)
- *working during lunch*
worth one's salt (to be)
- *to be of value*
written all over someone/thing (to be)
- *to be reflected in; to symbolize*

# Y

Yanks (the)
- *the New York Yankees baseball team; the Yankees*
yes-man (a)
- *one who always agrees with the boss*
You bet.
- *Sure. Absolutely. Definitely.*
You do the math.
- *The conclusion is obvious.*

You don't get a second chance to make a first impression.
- *You get one chance to succeed.*

You know the drill.
- *You know what to do; you get the picture.*

You snooze, you lose.
- *If you wait too long, you will lose an opportunity, etc.*

## Z

zero hour (to be)
- *the time something important begins; crunch time; high noon*

zero-sum gain (a)
- *a winner and a loser with no net change of wealth/advantages, etc.*

## Famous Movie and TV Quotes

"Failure is not an option." (pg. 69)
- *failure is unacceptable*
- *from the movie Apollo 13; 1995*

high noon (pg. 108)
- *crunch time; zero hour*
- *from the movie High Noon; 1952*

"I think this is the beginning of a beautiful friendship." (pg. 151)
- *from the movie Casablanca; 1942*

"I'm going to make him an offer he can't refuse." (pg. 28)
- *an offer that cannot be refused without risking certain death*
- *from the movie The Godfather; 1972*

"Is that your final offer?" (pg. 21)
- *from the UK TV game show Who Wants to be a Millionaire? 1998*

The $64,000.00 question (pg. 8, 43)
- *the big question*
- *from the TV game show The $64,000.00 Question; 1955-58*

"Toto, I have a feeling we're not in Kansas anymore." (pg. 141)
- *the realization that you have entered a strange new world*
- *from the movie The Wizard of Oz; 1939*

## Numbers

24/7
- *24 hours x 7 days a week; working non stop*

401K (a)
- *an employee investment plan wherein the employee's buying of stock is matched by the employer*

$64,000.00 dollar question (the)
- *the big question; the critical question*

800-pound gorilla (the)
- *the dominant player in a market*

## Shakespearean Idioms-Phrases (S)

All that glitters is not gold. (S)
- *Don't judge a book by its cover.*

All the world's a stage. (S)
- *Life is theater and we are all actors.*

All's well that ends well. (S)
- *everything is fine; no problem*

budge not an inch (to) (S)
- *to refuse to move/change*

cruel to be kind (to be) (S)
- *to cause pain for a beneficial effect*

go against the grain (to) (S)
- *to go in the opposite direction; to go against accepted practices*

go on a wild-goose chase (to) (S)
- *to waste time searching in the wrong direction*

hob knob (to) (S)
- *to schmooze; to rub elbows with; to socialize*

in a pickle (to be) (S)
- *in a difficult situation; in a quandary*

in my heart of hearts... (S)
- *to know deep within your heart/ soul*

It is all Greek to me. (S)
- *I have no idea.*

let sleeping dogs lie (to) (S)
- *to leave alone to avoid trouble*

make short shrift of (to) (S)
- *to do away with quickly*

method to [one's] madness [a] (S)
- *having a clear M.O. when one is thinking outside the box; having a good reason for acting in a seemingly irrational way*

strange bedfellows (to be) (S)
- *an unusual/unexpected association*

the be-all and the end-all (S)
- *the best; a paragon*

the green-eyed monster (S)
- *jealousy*

There's the rub. (S)
- *That is the problem/the issue.*

To be or not to be, that is the question. (S)
- *To do it or not. That is the $64,000.00 question.*

to thine own self be true (S)
- *Take care of yourself first.*

too much of a good thing (S)
- *negative consequences arising from enjoying something for too long*

tower of strength (to be a) (S)
- *to be a symbol of power/resolve*

What's done is done. (S)
- *It cannot be undone/changed; it is water under the bridge.*

## Acronyms

ASAP - *as soon as possible*
B.A. - *Bachelor of Arts*
B.A.A. - *Bachelor of Applied Arts*
BD - *bank draft*
BEP - *break even point*
B.F.A. - *Bachelor of Fine Arts*
BO - *branch office*
BOD - *board of directors*
BR - *branch*
B.Sc. - *Bachelor of Science*
B2B - *business to business*
B2C - *business to consumer*
CA - *chartered accountant*
CAO - *chief accounting officer*
CC - *carbon copy*
CD - *certificate of deposit*
CEO - *chief executive officer*
CFA - *chartered financial analyst*
CFO - *chief financial officer*
CIA - *certified internal auditor*

CIO - *chief information officer*
CMO - *chief marketing officer*
COB - *close of business*
COD - *cash on delivery*
COO - *chief operating officer*
CPC - *cost per click*
CSO - *chief security officer*
CTO - *chief technology officer*
CTQ - *critical to quality*
DINK - *dual income no kids*
DUI - *driving under the influence of alcohol*
EOE - *equal opportunity employer*
EVP - *executive vice president*
FAQ - *frequently asked questions*
FSU - *Florida State University*
FT - *full time*
FYI - *for your information*
GAAP - *generally accepted accounting principles*
GNP - *gross national product*
GP - *general partner*
G - *a grand (one thousand)*
HR - *human resources*
IOU - *I owe you*
IPO - *initial public offering*
IRS - *Internal Revenue Service*
IT - *internet technology*
J.D. - *law degree; Juris Doctorate*
JFK - *John F. Kennedy Int'l. Airport*
LAX - *Los Angeles Int'l. Airport*
LC - *letter of credit*
LLC - *limited liability company*
LL.M. - *Masters in International law; Legum Masters)*
LSU - *Louisiana State University*
M.B.A. - *Master of Business Administration*
M.F.A. - *Master of Fine Arts*
MO - *modus operandi*
MOR - *middle of the road*
M.Sc. - *Master of Science*
MSRP - *manufacturer's suggested retail price*
NA - *not available*
NDA - *non disclosure agreement*
NIMBY - *not in my backyard*
NP - *notary public*
NSF - *not sufficient funds*
NYC - *New York City*

NYSE - *New York Stock Exchange*
NYU - *New York University*
P - *president*
PA - *power of attorney*
PD - *per diem*
POD - *pay on delivery*
P&L - *profit and loss*
PLC - *product life cycle*
POS - *point of sale*
POV - *point of view*
PR - *public relations*
PSF - *price per square foot*
PT - *part time*
Q - *quarter*
QC - *quality control*
O - *officer*
OD - *officer and director*
OEM - *original equipment manufacturer*
ROI - *return on investment*
RVSP - *respond please*
SOHO - *small office/home office*
SUNY - *State University of New York*
SUV - *sport utility vehicle*
TBA - *to be announced*
TLC - *tendering-loving care*
TM - *trademark*
UConn - *University of Connecticut*
UMass - *University of Massachusetts*
USC - *University of Southern California*
USD - *U.S. dollars*
USP - *unique selling point*
VAT - *value-added tax*
VC - *venture capital*
V.P. - *vice president*
VIP - *very important person*
YUPPIE - *young urban professional*

## State　　　Abbreviation　Code

| State | Abbreviation | Code |
|---|---|---|
| Alabama | Ala. | AL |
| Alaska | Alaska | AK |
| Arizona | Ariz. | AZ |
| Arkansas | Ark. | AR |
| California | Calif. | CA |
| Colorado | Colo. | CO |
| Connecticut | Conn. | CT |
| Delaware | Del. | DE |
| Dist. of Columbia | D.C. | DC |
| Florida | Fla. | FL |
| Georgia | Ga. | GA |
| Hawaii | Hawaii | HI |
| Idaho | Idaho | ID |
| Illinois | Ill. | IL |
| Indiana | Ind. | IN |
| Iowa | Iowa | IA |
| Kansas | Kans. | KS |
| Kentucky | Ky. | KY |
| Louisiana | La. | LA |
| Maine | Maine | ME |
| Maryland | Md. | MD |
| Massachusetts | Mass. | MA |
| Michigan | Mich. | MI |
| Minnesota | Minn. | MN |
| Mississippi | Miss. | MS |
| Missouri | Mo. | MO |
| Montana | Mont. | MT |
| Nebraska | Nebr. | NE |
| Nevada | Nev. | NV |
| New Hampshire | N.H. | NH |
| New Jersey | N.J. | NJ |
| New Mexico | N.M. | NM |
| New York | N.Y. | NY |
| North Carolina | N.C. | NC |
| North Dakota | N.D. | ND |
| Ohio | Ohio | OH |
| Oklahoma | Okla. | OK |
| Oregon | Ore. | OR |
| Pennsylvania | Pa. | PA |
| Puerto Rico | P.R. | PR |
| Rhode Island | R.I. | RI |
| South Carolina | S.C. | SC |
| South Dakota | S.D. | SD |
| Tennessee | Tenn. | TN |
| Texas | Tex. | TX |
| Utah | Utah | UT |
| Vermont | Vt. | VT |
| Virginia | Va. | VA |
| Washington | Wash. | WA |
| West Virginia | W.Va. | WV |
| Wisconsin | Wis. | WI |
| Wyoming | Wyo. | WY |

# Famous Business Quotes

"The dictionary is the only place where success comes before work."

*Mark Twain, writer, humorist, lecturer*

"If you can dream it, you can do it."

*Walt Disney, co-founder of Walt Disney Productions*

"Any color—so long as it's black."

*Henry Ford, founder of the Ford Motor Company*

"We're not in the hamburger business. We're in show business."

*Ray Kroc, co-founder of McDonald's*

"If I had nine hours to chop down a tree, I'd spend the first six sharpening my axe."

*Abraham Lincoln, president 1861-1865*

"I had to make my own living and my own opportunity! But I made it! Don't sit down and wait for the opportunities to come. Get up and make them!"

*Madam C. J. Walker (born Sarah Breedlove); creator of beauty products; the first female and African-American self-made millionaire.*

"I made a resolve then that I was going to amount to something if I could. And no hours, nor amount of labor, nor amount of money would deter me from giving the best that there was in me. And I have done that ever since, and I win by it. I know."

*Colonel Sanders, founder of Kentucky Fried Chicken*

"Capital isn't that important in business. Experience isn't that important. You can get both of these things. What is important is ideas."

*Harvey Firestone, founder of Firestone Tires*

"Your time is limited, so don't waste it living someone else's life. Don't be trapped by dogma—which is living with the results of other people's thinking. Don't let the noise of others' opinions drown out your own inner voice. And most important, have the courage to follow your heart and intuition. They somehow already know what you truly want to become. Everything else is secondary."

*Steve Jobs, co-founder of Apple and Pixar*

"I failed in some subjects in exam, but my friend passed in all. Now he is an engineer in Microsoft and I am the owner of Microsoft."

*Bill Gates, founder of Microsoft*

"If your only goal is to become rich, you will never achieve it."

*John D. Rockefeller, founder of Standard Oil*

"High expectations are the key to everything."

*Sam Walton, founder of Wal-Mart*

"I have never known much good done by those who affected to trade for the public good."

*Adam Smith, writer, social philosopher*

"Many of life's failures are people who did not realize how close they were to success when they gave up."

*Thomas Edison, inventor, founder of General Electric*

"You do not lead by hitting people over the head—that's assault, not leadership."

*Dwight D. Eisenhower, president 1953-1961*

"An entrepreneur tends to bite off a little more than he can chew hoping he'll quickly learn how to chew it."

*Roy Ash, co-founder of Litton Industries*

"You are defined not by the answers you give but by the questions you ask."

*Bruce Stirling, writer*

"A business has to be involving, it has to be fun, and it has to exercise your creative instincts."

*Richard Branson, founder of the British Virgin Grp.*

"Well, you know, I was a human being before I became a businessman."

*George Soros, investor*

"If everything is under control, then you are going too slow."

*Mario Andretti, Grand Prix racing driver*

"The toughest thing about success is that you've got to keep on being a success."

*Irving Berlin, American song writer*

"Give me a couple of years and I'll make that actress an overnight success."

*Samuel Goldwyn, original Hollywood movie mogul; founder of Samuel Goldwyn Productions; co-founder of Famous Players and Metro-Goldwyn-Meyer (MGM)*

"If you can't explain it simply, you don't understand it well enough."

*Albert Einstein*

"If you would like to know the value of money, try to borrow some."

*Benjamin Franklin, politician, inventor, scholar*

"Every employee rises to the level of his own incompetence."

*The Peter Principle*

"I'm not the smartest fellow in the world, but I can sure pick smart colleagues."

*Franklin D. Roosevelt, president 1933-1945*

"Tell the audience what you're going to say, say it; then tell them what you've said."

*Dale Carnegie, writer, self-improvement guru*

"If you have to ask how much it costs, you can't afford it."

*J. P. Morgan, financier, banker, founder of J.P. Morgan and Company now JPMorgan Chase & Co.*

"There's a sucker born every minute."

*P. T. Barnum, co-founder of The Barnum and Bailey Circus, The Greatest Show on Earth!*

"Never make a big decision without sleeping on it."

*Martha Stewart, founder of Martha Stewart Living Omnimedia*

"Neither a borrower nor a lender be."

*William Shakespeare, Hamlet, Act 1, Scene 3, Polonius giving advice to his son Laertes*

"I am like any other man. All I do is supply a demand."

*Alphonse (Al) Capone, Chicago gangster*

"It's All About the Benjamins."

*Title of the rap single from the album No Way Out by Sean John Combs (aka Diddy)*

"A mediocre idea that generates enthusiasm will go further than a great idea that inspires no one."

*Mary Kay Ashm, founder of Mary Kay Cosmetics*

"I believe that banking institutions are more dangerous to our liberties than standing armies."

*Thomas Jefferson, founding father, writer of the American Declaration of Independence, president 1801-1809*

"Greed is good."

*Gordon Gekko, in the movie Wall Street (1987)*

## Also by *Bruce Stirling*

**Scoring Strategies for the TOEFL® iBT**
**- A Complete Guide -**
Nova Press, Los Angeles, USA

**Scoring Strategies for the TOEFL® iBT**
**- A Complete Guide -**
App available @ www.benchprep.com

**Practice Tests for the TOEFL® iBT**
Nova Press, Los Angeles, USA

**Speaking and Writing Strategies**
**for the TOEFL® iBT**
Nova Press, Los Angeles, USA

**Speaking and Writing Strategies**
**for the TOEFL® iBT**
Chinese version published by
Foreign Language Teaching and Research Press
Beijing, China

**Speaking and Writing Strategies**
**for the TOEFL® iBT**
published by Prakash Books, New Delhi, India
available at uRead.com

**500 Words, Phrases and Idioms**
**for the TOEFL® iBT**
*plus* **Typing Strategies**
Nova Press, Los Angeles, USA

\* \* \*

Bruce Stirling's TOEFL apps and videos are available at benchprep.com.
Visit Bruce Stirling TOEFL Pro at facebook and at
www.toeflpro.blogspot.com.